Advance Praise

"*Ready to step into your highest potential?* The Commitments *reveals how to create a life of intentional design, leading you to everything you ever wanted.*"

—Selena Soo, creator of Impacting Millions

"*Are you truly enjoying your reality? If not, give Dr. T and her simple method a try. Dr. T is the most powerful and focused reality creator I have personally encountered. Her simple method has been profoundly life-changing for me and those I serve. Her simple question 'What do you want instead?' has brought me and countless others through any challenging moment, intentionally creating a better reality moment by moment. As Dr. T shares, life is meant to be simple and practical, and this streamlined guide can show you the way to simply and easily create a better reality.*"

—Jenny-Viva Collisson, MD, integrative physician

"Most of us want to be great—truly great—in life, love and legacy. By making a commitment with your Self, Dr. Tracy Thomas can help you make it happen."

"This is a powerful book that offers hope and encouragement, letting people know that they don't have to be victims of conditioned dysfunctional patterns. Dr. Tracy gives the reader simple, clear, pragmatic tools to empower them to move from unconscious reactivity to conscious intention and choice, thereby changing their future and the future of the world."

"Emotional science is the forefront of how we're going to evolve humanity and raise the level of the collective consciousness on this planet! Dr. T has provided an easy framework for those who want to bring their highest intentional capacity forward. As a fellow emotional scientist, I agree that it's *imperative that we embrace the idea that navigating our emotions is the real compass to greatness!"*

—Jena Rodriguez, transformational mentor, emotional scientist, and growth strategist

"Learning how to transform negative emotions into positive intentions is one of the essential elements needed to optimize health. Dr. Tracy provides the tools to dramatically shift your well-being in every area of your life. The Commitments *will help you increase your emotional intelligence and elevate your capacity to lead at the highest level."*

—Merrick Rosenberg, author of *The Chameleon* and *Which Bird Are You?*

"For those that want to optimize their health, learning how to transform negative emotions into positive intentions is one of the essential elements needed to optimize health. The tools provided in The Commitments *can make a dramatic shift in your overall well being and every area of your life."*

—Kyrin Dunston, MD, FACOG, Founder and Medical Director of The Hormone Club PC and Midlife Metabolism Institute and host of *The Hormone Prescription* podcast

"This book is a game-changer for people who want to be more productive instead of reactive. If you want to produce more and struggle less, The Commitments *will transform your life."*

—Justin Stenstrom, Editor-in-Chief of EliteManMagazine.com

"If you're looking to optimize your health, wealth, and success, the strategies provided in The Commitments *give you the way to do it, minus all the stress. Dr. Tracy is the best in the world at helping emotionally sensitive people build the emotional strength they need to succeed."*

—AJ Mihrzad, bestselling author and Founder of Online Supercoach

"Dr. T has done it again, making it easier for the most sensitive people to use their sensitivity as their greatest asset."

—Elena Herdieckerhoff, TEDx speaker, intuitive business coach, and Founder and CEO of Elena Herdieckerhoff Company

"Dr. Tracy's words evoke emotional insight and inspiration! She reaches in, at soul level, to provide the self-awareness and self-management needed to live a happy, healthy life. The Commitments *provides an emotionally intelligent roadmap to discovering that life worth living we all seek."*

—Amy Sargent, Executive Director of the Institute
for Social and Emotional Intelligence

"Dr. Tracy has done it again. Another paradigm shifting book that helps us turn the most challenging emotions into our greatest creations."

—Aurora Winter, MBA, bestselling author of
*Turn Words Into Wealth: Blueprint for Your
Business, Brand, and Book to Create Multiple
Streams of Income & Impact*

"Dr. Tracy Thomas' expertise in the field of emotional science is groundbreaking. This book gives you the tools to start putting that emotional science into practice."

—Jessica Riverson, CEO of The Feminine CEO

THE
COMMITMENTS

THE
COMMITMENTS

A STEP-BY-STEP GUIDE TO
PERSONAL TRANSFORMATION

DR. TRACY THOMAS

ELEVATE YOUR LIFE MEDIA

THE COMMITMENTS
A Step-by-Step Guide to Personal Transformation

ISBN   978-1-5445-2787-1   *Hardcover*

978-1-5445-2788-8   *Paperback*

978-1-5445-2665-2   *Ebook*

The Commitments *is dedicated to the team at Dr. Tracy Inc., who each day live out the big commitment that we all share: to elevate the intentionality of our society. As the top leaders in the field of emotional science and emotional training, our team inspires me with their commitment to transforming lives and the world we live in, by operating at the most elevated plane of intentionality of any individuals I've ever encountered. Their dedication is the very thing that allows all of our clients, their families, and our community of followers to make the transformation from a reactive life to an intentional one. They are not just a Dream Team come true, they are a Reality Team of the highest level.*

Contents

Foreword

—Kathryn Porritt, CEO Business Bravery, CEO Luxury Influencers

When I first met Dr. Tracy Thomas, she was already an award-winning scientist who had carved out an important niche for herself supporting emotionally sensitive people to unlock their inner strength—the world's first Emotional Scientist. But she hadn't fully stepped into her magnificence.

Not yet.

I'm the leading luxury brand strategist for personal brands, and from the moment I met Dr. T, I knew she was going to change the world. From day one, I saw that she already had the raw materials to extend her reach. She was accomplished, articulate, whip-smart, and driven by her passion to support emotionally sensitive people in living more intentionally. She was supporting celebrities, visionaries, and geniuses behind the scenes, offering them unique and utterly transformative methods for harnessing their emotions effectively. She was blazing trails...but perhaps a bit more quietly than she should have.

It was my absolute pleasure to help Dr. T turn up the volume and amplify her message, becoming a true luxury icon. And since then, she has continued to change lives through coaching and her emotional strength training programs, while also sharing her groundbreaking strategies through articles, speaking, and books like this one.

With *The Commitments*, Dr. T furthers her mission to teach emotionally sensitive people how to evolve and thrive, this time through an emotional training process that can change them at a constitutional level. If you're emotionally sensitive yourself—someone who feels everything deeply and fully—your life is about to change for the better. Everything she's written here will revolutionize how you can up-level yourself, using this metamorphic process designed to recondition you from reactive to intentional. Essentially, these pages contain the key to intentionally creating the life you want by transforming your emotional sensitivity into your best asset.

Dr. T knows that you possess an incredible gift of creativity, intelligence, and intuition. And when emotionally sensitive people like you combine this gift with drive, that leads to influence, wealth, success, and status. In the coming chapters, you'll start building a solid emotional foundation and watch as every area of life dramatically improves. By breaking free from the prison of uncontrollable emotions, you'll become the strongest version of yourself.

Sounds glorious, am I right? As someone who has watched Dr. T grow and thrive herself—bringing her radical and innovative techniques to the people who need them most—I can assure you *it will be.*

Committing to
The Commitments

IF YOU'RE LIKE MOST PEOPLE, THE THINGS YOU'RE committed to in your life are entirely wrong.

I don't say this to be harsh or mean. It's almost inevitable because most of what we've been taught by society—and by extension, what our parents taught us, and our grandparents before them—isn't right either.

What are you most committed to in life? Most people will say things like family, career, friends, pets, church, or a cause. On the surface, these are fine. But the problem is that many people come to these commitments through a combination of conditioning (what they were taught they should do with their lives) and reactivity (responding to the stresses of life, as opposed to actively choosing their path).

The writer Henry David Thoreau famously said, "The mass of men lead lives of quiet desperation." He meant that people are mainly going through the motions, not actively choosing their lives. Thoreau said this in 1849—sadly, even with countless advances since, our emotional state hasn't changed much in over a century and a half.

Well, I can tell you that you are holding this book in your hands because you know, innately, that life doesn't have to be an endless struggle and that you are capable of achieving much more. And that—gasp!—life can even be fun. You don't need to live a life of quiet desperation.

So let me introduce you to a concept that will revolutionize your life. It will help you move from struggle and frustration to purpose and joy. It will help you connect to your true Self—the one buried deep under everyone else's expectation and agendas for you (including the subconscious ones you hold for yourself), and it will transform your relationship to other people, especially those bonds that have been rife with dysfunction.

Get ready to learn The Commitments.

The Commitments boil down to a series of steps that help make the experience of being a human much easier. They are simple, foolproof, and can be implemented in any situation. They are a set of thoughts and behaviors that can transform your mental and physical health and elevate every part of your life.

Beyond being steps, they are also part of a process, meaning they are more powerful than the steps of an equation. Together, they will provide you with a new way to think about your life, your perceptions, and your conditioning.

You may be wondering how I created The Commitments and why you should go through the effort to learn and implement them. The answer is I know how effective these Commitments are because I used them myself to go from a life of stress and reactivity to one with a thriving career, personal life, and deep happiness.

Today, I'm a psychologist who's worked with people from all walks of life, including celebrities and Fortune 500 CEOs. I run a multi-million-dollar company, Dr. Tracy Inc., that provides emotional training to help elevate my clients' lives from reactivity into one of intentionality. I'm happily married to a wonderful man. But I came from humble beginnings, and my current success is no accident.

I am the product of teenage parents—my mother was sixteen when she gave birth to me, and my dad was nineteen. To say that they were not prepared for parenthood, either practically or emotionally, is an understatement. While there was a great deal of love in my family, I was also born into emotional patterns of reactivity, volatility, anxiety, and self-medicating, to name just a few.

As a child, I would watch my family members argue, shut down, and misunderstand each other. They were emotionally sensitive people, channeling their feelings of overwhelm and reactivity and turning them into destructive habits. As stressful as it could be, I also recognized from a young age that their perceptions were much more complicated than the reality occurring—more accurately, they were caught up in repeating patterns, and largely unaware of them. I began to study their emotions in a scientific, objective way.

But being aware of these patterns wasn't initially enough for me to change them. Just like my father had done, I ended up getting married and divorced a few times. I struggled with an eating disorder for years. Although I had a high-paying corporate job, I felt depressed, like I was putting on a performance all the time.

So I went back to the lessons of my childhood. I decided to make it my life's work to help people heal from these misperceptions and reactive patterns. I earned a PhD in psychology. Through my own experience and through working with hundreds of clients, The Commitments were born.

Over the years, my clients have called The Commitments magical, and I believe them to be magical as well. But I also know that things can feel magical when they were previously mysterious and difficult for us, and then become easy. You'll learn to create things on purpose, instead of accidentally.

Because everyone is creating, whether they recognize it or not.

This is the process that's always going on. And creating with difficulty is not necessary.

By practicing The Commitments, you'll also learn how to become an *Emotional Scientist*. That's a phrase I coined to describe the practice of observing emotions (yours and others') without having a knee-jerk reaction to them. Being an Emotional Scientist gives you the ability to choose how you will respond to a situation for your greatest benefit, and to stop letting other peoples' wayward emotions affect you.

The Commitments you will learn are:

1. Stay connected to your Self.

2. Be intentional, accurate, and factual in your speech with yourself and others.

3. Choose your intentions, and focus on your outcomes over your feelings.

4. Say and do only what will create your
    outcomes.

For now, I invite you to embrace these Core Commitments, to fully integrate them and live them. Know that they will lead you to an elevated life, and they will allow you to live your full potential in each moment. They will allow you to become a world-changing leader, simply by the way you live your life.

They will be The Commitments you make to those you care about and those you influence during your time on Earth. After you are gone, these are The Commitments you will pass down to your children, grandchildren, and everyone you've touched. *They are your legacy, and they can be your children's children's legacy.* They are a tremendous gift for you to receive, and they can help you create anything.

If something is painful, difficult, or unproductive, you'll know that you can come back to these basics. Use them to elevate yourself and your life out of the trenches, or if you're already happy with your life, to soar even higher.

Each Core Commitment works beautifully together and allows The Method to bestow its most incredible benefits. Be diligent about integrating each one into your life, and also enjoy the process of growing deeper into each Commitment and the fulfillment that it will bring to you each and every day.

Now, let's get started.

CHAPTER 1

The Foundation

The Concept of Conditioning

TO START OFF, I WANT TO EXPLAIN ONE OF THE MOST important concepts a person can understand about being human: *conditioning.*

You may be thinking something like, *Dr. T, I already know about that. It's the way people are taught to act around each other.* And while you're right, when I talk about conditioning, I'm taking a more expansive view. *I'm talking about the very nature of reality and how we perceive it—and why the way we were raised to view it is only a small part of the picture.*

The highest form of suffering is to know what you want and to be continually re-experiencing something you don't. While it may seem that there is no rhyme or reason to this, it occurs because people are individually and collectively conditioned to keep recreating the same things over and over again—because that's what they are familiar with. Even when things are bad and we know they don't work, the conditioning to keep doing it is very strong.

Conditioning is how human beings are receiving, learning, and sharing information from the moment they are born and throughout the rest of their lives. It's largely a social process, in which things get developed and reinforced over and over. And when you do something, it creates a likelihood that you will do it again.

Let's take a benign example. Since childhood, you've probably been conditioned to put on a pair of shoes before you leave the house. You don't have to put much thought into it, beyond selecting a pair. But the idea of wearing shoes isn't one you debate. And because you kept putting on shoes as a kid, you continued to do so every day.

Eventually, putting on shoes just became automatic. This is what I refer to as *programming.* Just as you can program a computer, you can also program yourself to do certain things, such as learning the quickest route to drive to work or memorizing a dance routine. While programming can get a bad rap, from a practical standpoint, it's beneficial because it allows you to conserve time and energy for more difficult tasks.

Both conditioning and programming on their own are neutral, but they can develop into both positive and negative forms.

Another important pair of concepts is *reaction* and *intention*. A reaction is how you respond to a given stimulus, especially when it's a conditioned response. Reactions typically feel stressful and may not even be about a particular stimulus itself. They don't necessarily get easier either because, if the negative reaction was there in the first place, it has the potential to continue aggravating you, keeping you stuck. You may not be aware of these reactive patterns, which makes them harder to change. In turn, this can keep you from building a life that is a reflection of what you really want and care about.

In contrast, intention is the opposite of reaction. It's the conscious choice of how you want to respond to a stimulus. Intentions usually feel good; they are reflective of your deepest desires and how you want to spend your life, both in the moment and in the grand scheme. While intentions initially can take some work, with practice, they become second nature.

The Commitments will teach you to set and keep intentions.

Okay, some big concepts here. But stick with me—we're going to delve more into how conditioning works, which will bring all these ideas into focus.

Let's start with perception and what's really going on in "reality."

Say there's a man walking down the street on a sunny day. He's middle-aged, of average height and weight. You ask three different people to describe the man. The first person, a teenaged girl, notes that he is wearing flip flops. The second person, an older gentleman, notices the man's body turning and says he's approaching his driveway. The third person, a young mother, states that he looks a little worried. All of these are just different perceptions of the same raw reality.

Each person's take is unique because we are each perceiving reality based on the millions of things we have perceived before in life—and the countless things human beings before us have perceived, stretching all the way back through the history of humanity. Anything created in the past—from small conversations to big discoveries, like Thomas Edison inventing the light bulb—has continuous momentum that is carried forward.

The way we perceive our surroundings is also a result of the perspective of the people around us. Their perceptions shape the way we view the world. This includes people in our immediate vicinity—such as spouses, children, or roommates—and through more remote channels like social media.

For most people, the sum total of their perception of reality creates a largely unconscious (and flawed) filter. *But when we know that this is a filter, and that we are simply **perceiving an experience**, we no longer have to use it as our only perception of what's going on.* We can instead choose any type of interpretation we want because we have the powerful creative capacity to do so.

In the case of the man walking down the street, you could notice that he is smiling and interpret that he's doing so because he loves the roses in front of his house. You can notice something totally different than you would have before.

This intelligence can guide you forward when you use what I call your *internal navigation system*. This is your inner wisdom; your inner GPS that gives your life direction, whether you choose to follow it or not. It urges you to follow your interests, talk to an intriguing person, and express the real you. You can access it by being in connection with your Self. Ideally, it's meant to guide you throughout your life so you can fulfill your unique purpose. The Commitments you're going to learn will shed more light on how to access this intelligence.

From the moment we are born, we begin to absorb the patterns and environment around us. Let's use the example of a newborn named Johnny. He starts to hear, see, touch, and feel the world around him. But in addition, he's experiencing emotions—both his own and the different emotions of the people around him. Johnny is a sponge soaking up what his parents and other caregivers feel, think, and believe, and how they do things. Much of this is not a conscious choice; it's just part of Johnny's human nature.

Johnny's parents try to create patterns for their baby, like when to eat and when to go to sleep in his crib. Johnny absorbs these patterns, just as he absorbs the rhythms of his mother or primary caretaker—how fast she moves, how present she is with him, how much she smiles.

Johnny's genes also have a role in his development—he has his dad's blue eyes, and he's left-handed like his mom. The way those genes express themselves is a set of rhythms for Johnny, but beyond that, his environment is shaping him.

Little Johnny becomes conditioned for whatever his parents do. If his dad is patient and soothing when he cries, he absorbs that. If his dad reacts to his crying by shouting and storming out of the room, he absorbs that too. His dad is having one version of reality, and his mom is having her own version of reality, and both realities are influencing Johnny. If it doesn't feel good to be in the presence of a particular person, Johnny is still dependent and captive to absorbing what is around him—especially when he's in this young, vulnerable state.

What's more, Johnny's patterns are also going into the environment and being absorbed by the rest of the family members so that the baby becomes part of that emotional ecosystem. Johnny and his parents are syncing up with each other.

Without meaning to, Johnny's mom and dad may teach him only to be connected with other people, not with himself. That sets up a scenario where Johnny may go through life propelled by everyone else's beliefs, especially those of his parents. As he gets older, there's great power in being aware of that and deciding if he wants to follow that programming or not.

Just like Johnny, you can replace whatever doesn't serve your true Self with new programming that creates a new set of outcomes. That's really fun and exciting, and alters the programming that says your whole life will be determined by your genetics and the circumstances you were born into, and that there's not much you can do to change that.

As Johnny develops as a child, where so much information is being cemented into his sense of Self, he will start to form beliefs. These could be any kind of belief—*brothers are fun, sisters are challenging. Anxiety is something you just have to live with. Ice cream makes me feel better.*

All of this programming creates his filter of the world around him. And just like Johnny, as you interact with people, you're joining their conditioning and patterns. The result is a unique process and rhythms.

That's why we want to be connected to ourselves and conscious of it so we can recognize things. There's a vast difference between Johnny yelling when he gets upset because that's what his dad does, and Johnny feeling the urge to yell, recognizing it, and choosing to take a deep breath. In the first case, he perpetuates his father's cycle; in the second, he intentionally creates his own.

COMMITMENTS QUESTION: What patterns in my life do I not like but find very hard to break?

Conditioning isn't just what we are taught as children. Johnny is going to grow up and take with him the perceptions from his childhood and those close to him as he starts to navigate the world as a teenager, and then as a young adult. He absorbs and processes all the stimuli in his environment so that he becomes what he is around, through every piece of learning that's happening socially and environmentally. As he takes in stimuli, he blends them with all his previous learnings.

When adult Johnny starts working with a new manager at a job, after several weeks, they've been around each other in a certain way. They may be friendly with each other, or the manager might be standoffish, or the manager might yell at Johnny for making a mistake, causing him to avoid the manager as much as possible. In any case, there becomes a pattern of how they operate and how they communicate with one another.

Just like Johnny, you also have patterns of which you can become aware. For example, let's say at 2:00 p.m. every day you find yourself distracted and shopping online instead of completing your work deadline, and you're having less-than-desirable job outcomes from that.

But you may not recognize that there is a whole sequence of things happening to create this pattern; it can possibly derive from everything that's occurred since you were born. Maybe shopping gives you a sense of control over life or a quick hit of pleasure because you didn't grow up with nice things. Or maybe the pattern is from having a certain set of friends in your life—you all express yourselves through clothes, and you shop to feel part of your friendship circle. But when you add one more friend, now there's a different flow because everything is now evolving.

Certain dynamics are being replaced with others, which creates a continuous alteration depending on yourself and who and what you're interacting with. Once you know these patterns, you can think about what you intend; for example, on Tuesdays from 2:00 p.m. to 3:00 p.m., you condition yourself to send an answer to every email in your inbox, instead of shopping online. Or you set up a daily check-in with your manager so you'll be busy then. There's an infinite field of possibilities of things to choose from and configure.

This sort of process is happening all the time, in everyone's life. It's important to understand how this works and to know that you can actually select how you want things to go.

LIVING IN A REACTIVE EXISTENCE

We all have knee-jerk reactions to things from time to time—but if this is how you live most of the time, it alters your reality, and not for the best. A reactive existence builds on itself and keeps people moving backwards, reliving pain, and being overstimulated because they've spent so much time reacting to things. What is going on outside of you begins to create a whole world inside of you, of struggle and chaos, that mirrors what you are taking from outside forces. This happens not just because of the stimulus itself, but because of your perception of the stimulus. This perception comes from your upbringing and the perceptions of those around you now, who are sharing those beliefs and interpretations. *Some people can live their entire life in a reactive pattern, never completely living.*

For example, when Johnny's dad shouts at him, it can cause Johnny to avoid his father as much as possible. As Johnny grows up, he doesn't know how to deal with anger effectively, so he either bottles it up or explodes just like dear old Dad. And his dad does this because it's the way his father dealt with feeling overwhelmed, and so on. While he doesn't necessarily enjoy shouting at his son, it gets the results he wants, and he doesn't feel compelled to change this pattern.

This creates and stores beliefs and information that can perpetuate generations of suffering, genetic health problems, and hereditary tendencies for issues such as addiction and depression. It's your comfort zone (even if that's really uncomfortable). In many families, we witness generations of people living out the same lives and issues from their ancestors—without even consciously choosing to do so.

When you are captive to your own programming, you can win the lottery and still end up getting the same outcomes you're familiar with. Money can't fix deeply ingrained patterns of stress, anger, and dysfunction; only you can. And people will recreate their current programming even in new circumstances, which is why they do things like reliving their same relationship struggles in a new relationship.

There are countless cycles occurring in the world, around us, and in our bodies—things that are sequenced to be happening in a certain rhythm and a certain order. As he becomes a teenager, Johnny is pre-programmed to go through puberty and start growing facial hair. We can influence nature as well. For example, when you regularly water your plants, they come to expect being watered at a certain time. It all becomes a lot of energetic processes going on that are not obvious to everyone.

Even though these processes aren't something you can see all the time, they exist. It's basic science and the rhythm of life. Though Johnny can't see gravity, it exists, as he'll find out when he's a toddler and falls off the couch.

Without even knowing it, we can be experiencing an infinite number of cycles connected to a tree that is growing outside our house, a weather pattern, or the patterns of the planets and things beyond that. Your entire physiology and emotional system run on these cycles.

In previous generations, there was only so much that people came into contact with. Some people had more stimuli in a big city as opposed to the country, and women were largely relegated to the home. But now with technology, we are all able to experience much more, and there's significantly more conditioning going on. If Johnny were born now, he'd know how to scroll through Mom's apps on her cell phone as a two-year-old, even though his ancestors couldn't even dream of the existence of a phone, let alone the "minicomputer" that is a smartphone.

For generations, people—and thinking of yourself, your specific ancestry—have been repeatedly experiencing certain things because that's what people do. They repeat patterns, mostly without awareness. *But you are not helpless against these patterns—when you are aware of them, you have a choice.*

Whatever is in the atmosphere is directing us and influencing us all the time. When you are aware of this, it allows you to really optimize your experience of life without living in what is typically a reactive existence. That's because most people are not aware of all the programs that are running and that they have taken in, and how they manifest: in their relationships, in their bank accounts, in their family systems, and in their evolution as a person.

The funny thing is, feeling frustrated can feel so vulnerable to people that it creates a desperation in them, and they actually end up doing *more* of what they don't want to do in a cycle that goes on and on. But this doesn't just affect the person in question: for every human that is struggling in reactive conditioning, every other human is impacted because we are all interconnected. That's why The Commitments are important for you to live and display to others—*when even one more person is in an intentional state, every other human on the planet benefits from that.* For every intention a person lives from, there is more possibility available for everyone.

The Commitments will teach you to become connected to your Self. And when you become connected with your Self, you seek to be present to everything that occurs around you. In a more present state of awareness, you can position your attention further *into* something to be more connected, or *out* of something. You can lower something down the hierarchy with your attention, prioritizing something else so that you get to experience what you want. This is true even in a scenario where another person is experiencing something else and may or may not know that they are choosing to experience that.

For example, let's say you're waiting to pay for something at the store. The person checking out has a complicated return to process, and the line is piling up behind you. The woman in front of you is impatient—she keeps sighing and tapping her foot, looking around for another employee to open another register. You start to feel annoyed by the wait too, until you realize that it isn't the cashier's fault, and you aren't in a hurry anyway. If the woman in front of you were to actively choose her experience, she'd probably feel the same, instead of her automatic irritation.

This is very important because most people don't know whether they are consciously choosing or not. *And if you're not consciously choosing, without meaning to, you're unconsciously choosing—you're experiencing anything that comes up as a conditioned reaction.*

Just as you experience these conditioned responses that are difficult and full of suffering, you can also keep shifting until you train yourself for a different, more productive experience. You'll get to the point at which you'll interact with the same stimulus but have a different conditioned response. And if you don't like that response, you can shift any of your reactions into a new intention at any moment.

The truth is that we all have the power to change our responses. That is an incredible foundation for living life in the most conscious way.

It also means understanding that there are many cycles going on that require your attention in the present moment to what you are intending. Without recognizing this fully, you can simply end up reacting in a conditioned way. But with practice, you can be stable with your attention and intentions so that you go down your own path of outcomes without constantly feeling disturbed and forced to pull yourself onto another track that may not be your agenda.

When you become aware of programming, you can program your own Self and condition yourself for programs that you want to run within to carry out the things you want to create in your life.

The goal is to take the programs that are often activated without your knowledge and replace them with a deliberate program that simplifies the experience of being a person—the process of being a powerful creator. You can shift from a reactive existence to a connected, intentional one that creates the outcomes that you intend, and even something better.

You can have a truly elevated existence through your intentions, aware of any stimulus, able to consider it, and stay connected to what you're doing. You can train yourself not to go off track because you're fully committed to creating your vision. And you can do it over and over and over again so that, just like driving a car, you eventually don't have to think about it.

You want to utilize your capacity to coach yourself in any moment you need to make decisions and select in a way that gives you the best outcomes. Because otherwise you are essentially in an alternate reality, unaware of your own Self and all of the forces shaping you.

It's also really important to be aware of the reality that other people are creating with their conditioning and intentions.

Everyone operates with a certain set of beliefs that make up a particular framework, whether they realize it or not. You may be successful in some areas of life but struggle in others, and you're not sure why. For example, let's say you have a loving marriage and close friends, but your whole life, money has been a struggle. You may consciously believe that you are always going to struggle with money, or you may not even be aware of this belief. Maybe your parents struggled to make ends meet, and your friends' parents did too. Everyday (but unexpected) expenses—like a car needing new brakes or when you got braces—created a tremendous amount of stress in your family, so you internalized that money is a stressful aspect of life that is difficult to control.

And yet, this is simply a belief. As an adult, you have the power to change these beliefs, and through them, your circumstances. Instead of seeing it as a negative, if you believe that money is a tool to help you create the life you want, and that you are capable of earning so you can live comfortably, you will create that reality in the world. You will be open to opportunities to make money using your existing skills or expand your skills to generate more income. You will be truly receiving what is accessible to you and what you are capable of creating. And this positive momentum keeps building on itself.

COMMITMENTS QUESTION: What does my conditioning have me programmed to do?

- Positive conditioning (e.g., self-care)

- Negative conditioning (e.g., stressing over money)

This is part of the major work of The Method and The Commitments that comprise it: to shift this pattern so that everything you do is a conscious choice that you can operate from for yourself, and that you can share with your family and everyone with whom you interact. Instead of everyone functioning on their own broken framework, this creates a shared framework that eliminates the unhealthy patterns.

The Commitments allow you to take all of the information you experience, perceive, and receive, and run it through this set of steps that allow you to be working on an intentional basis instead of a reactive one. Doing this over and over, you become conditioned for what it is you want to do and experience. You are attuned to how you want to feel and how to manifest this to your specifications as a person, all while being high-functioning in your interactions with everything and everyone.

While this may sound like a tall order, in truth, this is part of our purpose here on Earth. We have not been given a practical, simple method for how to live a life full of potential, minus the suffering. I know people believe and many religions teach that suffering is a necessary part of life, but I believe it is completely optional when we change ourselves to function at our highest level.

You may wonder how you stand out from everyone else in a world of almost 8 billion people. But the truth is *everyone is programmed to operate from the uniqueness of who they are.* You are, in fact, programmed to bring us what we're supposed to know from you, your expertise, and contribution into the evolution of the human family.

For some people, all of their conditioning can work well so that they feel like their life is really a reflection of who they are. They feel fulfilled, secure, and like they are contributing. But conditioning can also counter what they innately want as a unique person, making it hard for the person to be themselves and be the most productive they can be. Think of a gay or lesbian teenager who is told their attraction to the same sex is "just a phase," so he or she has to deny part of who they are (which never really works, does it?).

Our higher Self really is here to choose and to create. The purpose of life is simply to be yourself, to share the contributions that are already pre-programmed into you when you come into the world. Does that sound trite or like it's too easy? As we've discussed, being yourself is actually quite a challenge because of the way we've been conditioned. It takes practice to start tuning into yourself and courage to share who you really are. But once you start, there's no turning back—you won't want to operate any other way.

When we are really connected to ourselves, we know what we're supposed to do.

When you have this next-level awareness operating, you get to choose what you want to align with and carry forward into your existence. You get to choose what you want to believe, the perception you want to focus on, and what reality you want to create from any moment that is occurring in your life.

The purpose of life is also to receive everyone else's expertise. We get to share the reality we want with other people who also want that reality, and to create realities together—which is *co-creating*. You want to co-create with people to build strong families, work relationships, friendships, and other essential ties. You can do this by helping other people live from their intentions as well. You can interact with others so that you'll be able to see their patterns, and not make everything so emotional and personal. And you can be aware and then direct yourself according to intentions, instead of what happens in much of society, where reactive conditioning in another person creates reactions in everyone around them.

We're ultimately experiencing billions of versions of people's realities—those who are here in this world and even beyond to those in generations past, as far as humankind goes. Especially through the internet, we are now sharing these realities at an exponential pace—through every post, picture, image, and word online.

And from a purpose perspective, understand that everything that is in our atmosphere also plays into our development as a being and shapes us. You can be aware of that and decide how you want it to shape you and what you want to do.

WHY MOST OF US LIVE OUTSIDE OF PURPOSE

Have you noticed that some people seem to find it easy to express their purpose and work from their intentions? Rock stars, scientists researching cures to diseases, and the Kardashians all seem to be pretty intentional about their lives, regardless of how you feel about their contributions to society. These people are essentially setting the agenda for everyone else too. Because the more intentional and capable someone is, the more likely that they get to lead and influence others.

At the same time, when people are in longstanding reaction patterns, and they don't fully understand them—or what they understand isn't enough to help them make a change—they can become unintentionally influential in creating things that they *didn't* intend to create in their life and in the lives of other people. This tends to result in a lot of suffering. And part of why people end up having so many challenges is because there are so many impulses coming up. We even have avoidance patterns—things we're conditioned to think are difficult—like *I can't do math* or *I'll never get in shape.*

We're normally creating on some version of auto-pilot, which is good when the autopilot is what we want, like making it easy and pleasant to take a shower every morning. But we then perceive it as bad when the autopilot creates something we don't want, like dreading going to our jobs on Monday morning. However, this autopilot is just a piece of programming, where you might not know why you want something but keep creating something else—like leaving one job you don't like for another that you ultimately end up disliking too. That's why it's so important to be connected to your intentions; otherwise, other people's intentions will happen instead of your own. And then you end up experiencing a combination of intentionality and reactivity, which is what most people live in.

You keep experiencing this because there's momentum for it, sometimes stretching back centuries. What has already occurred will keep occurring until you become highly, consciously aware of it and can choose if that's what you want to continue experiencing—or if you choose a different intention and select a new outcome and a new reality that you would like to create, in any moment.

We have to recognize that no matter how significant the momentum, if we want something to change, ultimately if we're willing to focus on it repeatedly, it will shift into its new version within a fairly short period of time. And the longer that goes on, eventually it will become automated. This can often be the case when someone tries to quit smoking; the nicotine withdrawal symptoms like headache, hunger, and fatigue rage when they first quit, but if they can ride it out for a few weeks, the symptoms subside and get easier, and ultimately are gone.[1]

In reality, we are here to be productive in life rather than to create more pain and difficulty. So understanding programming and conditioning is important. Some people make this very personal, thinking, *Why do other people get to have more than I do?* But it's really more about learning how life operates and how to succeed, which The Method can do for you.

---

1 Gina Shaw, "Surviving Without Smoke: Month 1," WebMD, accessed December 10, 2020, https://www.webmd.com/smoking-cessation/first-month-not-smoking#1.

COMMITMENTS QUESTIONS: What does my navigation tell me I should do with my life? Am I close or far off from this currently?

Does it feel a little intimidating to know that you're creating your reality, whether you're aware of it or not? Especially if some aspects of your life are not how you want them to be, this may feel discouraging. But the truth is that this knowledge is positive.

For years, adult Johnny has been afraid that he will turn into his dad—blowing up over the slightest little thing, creating a reality where he is distanced from the people he loves. But this is not Johnny's destiny; he realizes that he can choose to pause when he feels upset and examine his emotions, instead of acting on them. And in this way, he can create better relationships with those he cares about.

This is a crucial shift because it puts you in the powerful, creative capacity you already exist in so that you don't keep creating what you don't intend to. Instead, your capacity can create exactly what you intend to because you're living in an intentional connected state of being that just becomes the way you operate. It replaces the reactive process.

Most of us have some really good patterns and rhythms, and others that are very painful and uncomfortable. In some cases, people feel desperate to change their circumstances but don't have the concept of how to go about the process. By understanding how conditioning works and how to take ownership of it, you become completely present in the driver's seat of what is happening in the moment. Your attention can be in the present and also be creating the future, rather than feeling burdened by the past and overwhelmed by stimuli in the present.

The difference between reactivity and intentionality is the difference between being destructive and being productive. That's critical to our world right now because every single person needs to be creating intentionally and bringing forth their contribution. They wouldn't be here to give it if they weren't supposed to be. Every person is needed to create the world we want it to be, in a way that works for everyone.

Every reaction and negative process that happens to a person and every pattern that they stay stuck in—whether it's a pattern of poverty, violence, over-spending, or under-supporting themselves and under-enjoying life—impacts the entire world because we are all in the exact same field together. And it's more important than ever for people to recognize their epic level of influence on everything. Truth be told, we are all affected by every one of our intentions and reactions.

Taking a step back from your patterns and conditioning is actually simpler than it may seem. You can do that by becoming an *Emotional Scientist*, as I mentioned before. By which I mean scientifically observing the conditioning that surrounds you, rather than just being confused and negatively impacted by it. When your programming isn't leading you to the outcomes you want, it doesn't mean you've failed. That's just how you know the programming isn't working for you anymore.

What do scientists do? They study things, observe them, test them out. When something isn't working, they adjust their method and try again.

Just like a scientist, if you can study your emotions and patterns rather than just being affected by them, and observe them while being fully present, that allows you to see what conditioning is unfolding in the moment. That way you can reprogram yourself to be reflective of exactly what it is you want to create, who you really are, the way you want to be, and your deeper purpose here.

COMMITMENTS QUESTION: Do I believe I am capable of change?

Let's say Johnny wants to get married, but his relationships with women keep failing. He starts to examine when each relationship ended, and the common thread is that he had a fight with a girlfriend and then she broke up with him. He starts to wonder if the way he argues with a partner is the root of the problem. In his next relationship, he becomes more observant of himself when he gets upset and how he talks to his girlfriend. Johnny learns how to disagree without exploding, and his relationship flourishes, allowing him to reach his intention of being happily married.

I'm inviting you to practice The Method and know you are replacing a framework of mass reference that most people aren't even aware of. Know that everything you've ever absorbed creates an impact—everything you've ever read, watched, heard, observed, or remembered. When we follow The Method, we decide where we put our attention and what *intention* we have with our attention. That way, our influence on ourselves and everyone around us—and the reverberating effect of each person—can be positive and consistently felt around the world as an elevating process for our human family.

None of us can fully and truly escape the exact world that is going on, nor should we, but we get to create our own unique reality within the entire reality of the planet. We can condition ourselves out of pain by conditioning ourselves through intentionality and essentially reprogramming ourselves for anything.

Get ready to have a major shift of your entire emotional foundation into one that supports you to create your specific outcomes. But also recognize that while you experience this training, all of your previous programs are still running, as we embark on a deeper journey into being able to shift your current conditioning.

With that, let's delve into the first Commitment.

CHAPTER 2

Commitment One

Stay Connected to Your Self

"This above all—To thine own self be true."

—*Hamlet*, Act I, Scene 3, by William Shakespeare

THERE IS ONE COMMITMENT YOU NEED ABOVE ALL others: stay connected to your Self. By Self, I mean the deepest part of you, the one that's below all the noise and chaos of the world that jostles you around. It's the part of you that's still there at the end of a busy day, thinking back on all you've done. And it's the part of you that can guide you in intense times.

Why does this matter so much? First, because you have to create a relationship with your Self. That naturally requires a deep connection with yourself. But even more importantly, being connected to your Self is *the state you're meant to be in*. You're meant to operate from this emotionally elevated state all the time, not just when you're sitting on a beach listening to the waves (although there's nothing wrong with that scenario).

And once you're in connection with your Self, you want to stay connected to your Self. Because without being and remaining connected to your Self, you can feel all kinds of stress, struggle, and difficulty. As we discussed about conditioning, when you're out of tune with your Self, you can be in reactive cycles and patterns and not even be aware of them.

We've already talked some about reactivity. When you're in reactivity, you're allowing life to happen *to* you, instead of you being connected to life. You're a passenger in life, versus being in the flow of life. But when you are connected to your Self and the energy around you, you can orchestrate what goes on with all of the energy you encompass—and the energy that's available to you in the entire world, from the planet itself.

You may be thinking, *Sure, Dr. T, that sounds great. But how am I supposed to connect to my Self, let alone do it all the time?* It will take some practice, but it's really more like learning a good habit. Just as your parents probably taught you to brush your teeth when you were young, and now it's an ingrained habit that requires very little effort (and no one has to tell you to do it).

The steps of this Commitment are to:

1. Connect to your Self.

   In every moment of your life, pay attention to how you're truly feeling and what you're really wanting. You might notice how happy you feel when you get to spend a lazy afternoon with your kids. Or you might notice that spending time with a friend whose company you used to enjoy now feels draining.

2. Continually stay connected to your Self.

   Once you start checking in with your Self, the trick is to keep doing so. It can be tricky when you get busy or when you're dealing with difficult emotions. But keep up the discipline of noticing how you feel in different situations.

3. Constantly check in with your Self to see whether you're in a reaction or an intention.

    When you check in with your Self often, you will start to notice that sometimes you're acting very deliberately—you're going to buy flowers for a sick friend or calling your mom for Mother's Day. But other times, you may be reacting to what's happening; your spouse is snappy, so you're short too.

4. Examine if you're in the effect of an unconscious emotional cycle that's repeating and taking you along with it.

    Many of our reactions are actually patterns that we keep cycling through. Your dad was frequently critical of you growing up, so you still get defensive around him even as an adult.

5. Examine if you're connected to your intentions and collaborating with the world to create exactly what you want.

Think back again to the beginning of the process—what is it that you're actually wanting in a situation? If you're looking to land your dream job, are you focused on exactly what that will look like, or just going to any interview you can get?

When you practice this process regularly, ultimately your conditioning becomes that you are in a completely connected state, and you are consistently self-aware and aware of everything around you. And you are conditioned to create the reality that you want to create, rather than just being in a default setting where everything in the world is in constant motion of impacting you.

To connect with your Self, you simply check in with your Self often—as often as you check your smartphone. I use this as an example because it's one of the foremost ways people are currently conditioned to operate.

Just as you regularly scan your phone for messages and scroll through it for information, check in with your Self. Become a person who is constantly scanning yourself, checking in with every single molecule of motion that is occurring within yourself and within your environment, to be able to recognize what is occurring when it's occurring. Notice how you're feeling, what you're thinking, the people and things around you, what you're wanting in that moment, and how close or far your reality is from that. If you're driving, you might notice how you feel about the driving conditions, what's going through your mind as you go through traffic, the roads and sights around you, and how you feel about your destination.

Okay, so let's say you check in with your Self. You are feeling good. Great! Keep on with what you're doing. But let's say you feel negative emotions or a mix of good or bad emotions, as people frequently do. No sweat—instead of ignoring the emotions, try digging a little deeper to understand them.

When you start to feel a negative emotion, discern whether it's:

- Something obviously stressful (a negative energetic charge that is a painful part of programming)

- Something you're picking up from your environment and the people in it (transference)

- Something from before that may not be obvious but causes stress now (previous conditioning that's affecting your ability to process what's within your environment now)

Say someone cuts you off when you're driving in heavy traffic. You start to feel anger and stress boil up inside of you. This negative charge may simply be because you had to slam on your brakes to avoid an accident (something obviously stressful). But if you check in with your Self and dig a bit deeper, you may be picking up the emotional chaos of the person who cut you off, as well as the irritation of the driver behind you who had to slam on his breaks too (transference). In addition, perhaps you were told as a teenager that you weren't a good driver, so even now as an adult you feel unduly stressed when something erratic happens behind the wheel, even though this event isn't your fault and you responded well.

Transference can be tricky because we're wired to be social beings, and we don't want to simply ignore the emotions of others. And, say if your baby is crying, you certainly want to address her upset emotions. But with adults, it often doesn't help us to take on their emotions.

Here's another example: let's say you have some neighbors who drink too much every Saturday night and wind up arguing loudly on their porch. You may inadvertently find yourself feeling angrier and more stressed with your own spouse on Sunday mornings because you've absorbed the neighbors' emotions and they are lingering in you. Assuming that your neighbors are not abusing one another, there's no reason for you to get involved—and no reason to take on their emotions. Instead of getting "stuck" in their energy yourself, what's most helpful is to elevate your own frequency by releasing these emotions in yourself and living in your own intentions. By raising your own frequency, you raise the collective frequency—which is actually the best way to help your neighbors too.

COMMITMENTS QUESTIONS: As I spend more time connected to my deepest Self, what do I notice? Am I generally happy, anxious, etc.?

When you check in with your Self regularly, there becomes an awareness of what's occurring right now. And the most important thing you can know when you check in with your Self is to be able to understand if you're in a pattern of reaction or intention. Are you reacting—where you're in a negative form of the experience of yourself and your environment that you exist in—or are you connected and in intentionality, harnessing all of the energy that is within you, within your environment, and ultimately running through all things in the world and in the universe?

Let's go back to the example of being cut off in heavy traffic. If you are in *intention*, you might mentally note what happened, acknowledge that you did a good job responding, and then think about how you're in transit to the grocery store to buy yourself and your family nourishing food. If you are in *reaction*, you might say, "How dare that person cut me off! This is *my* street!" You could feel rattled and stressed throughout the whole rest of your drive, and your bad mood might extend to your entire time at the grocery store, where you snap at the cashier. Basically, you are unaware of how dynamic your environment is and that you're not separate from it.

See how you can have two vastly different experiences of the exact same stimulus? It all boils down to how you're approaching life: through reaction or intention.

If you find you're in reaction, it's okay. This isn't a test you failed. We can get overstimulated by our environment and be constantly reacting to it, swept up and captivated, becoming conditioned for it and shaping our cycles to be stressful, negative ones. But you also have the option to focus your attention on intention—using your powerful, creative capacity to focus your energy into outcomes that you want. Which sounds better to you?

Whether you're aware of it or not, *this is actually how life works all the time; at any given moment, you're either in an intention or a reaction.* Being connected to your Self will help you to understand—are you in pattern, or are you in purpose?

COMMITMENTS QUESTIONS: Do I spend more time in reaction or intention? How easy is it for me to shift into intention?

If you are in a reaction, you have the potential to re-experience further reactivity cycles that you are not even aware of, let alone the cycles you are aware of that are more obvious. You could be making decisions large and small that will carve out your path in life and keep you from living your potential. It will be the process of either repeating cycles of struggle that are happening to you unconsciously or being able to completely use your creative capacity to be in the driver's seat of your Self and your life.

This is where people become afraid and even traumatized because most people are not taught from the beginning of their life (or really any time in life) how to be connected with themselves. When you become connected to your Self and stay connected as a continual commitment, you can observe and experience a complete, multi-dimensional experience of reality that is much more objective.

How can you break a cycle of reactivity, especially if you don't know what's causing it? By being connected to the fact that the cycle is occurring and harnessing it into intentional patterns and outcomes. And by doing that over and over again, until it becomes the new way of being. It's an awesome responsibility, but also incredibly empowering because it puts you squarely in your powerful, creative capacity—one that many people may never even recognize or ever become truly adept at using.

If we don't recognize all of the cycles that are occurring and become attuned to what is going on, the challenge is that reaction patterns can look very much like intention patterns.

For example, let's say someone texts you a question on your smartphone, and you feel compelled to respond right away. It's good to help people and communicate with them, of course. But if you're not in a connected state with your Self, you're not actively choosing your response to that text message; it's just a reaction. We see this with people who are compulsively on their phones, reacting to every piece of stimuli on their device as a conditioned response.

Immediately responding to the text could appear to be an intentional process, but it's really a reactive one if it's causing you to lose time and not be connected to your Self and the purposes that are priorities to you. When we are not connected to ourselves, we are in a process that is much more "wear and tear" because we are in the passenger seat and someone else is driving. We are just reacting to what they are directing rather than steering with our own directions, which can only come from being truly connected to ourselves and asking ourselves whether we are in an intention or a reaction.

Let's say you recognize that you are not in intention when you're responding to a text message. Fine. Ask yourself: what is your intention? That way, you can become reconnected to the answer and let that clarity drive your intentions forward with a focus on creating the outcomes that come from your unique directions. If the answer is that you intend to work for ninety minutes without interruption to make progress on an important project, it's okay to put your phone away and respond to texts later.

When you find that you're in a reaction, simply ask: **what's my intention?** The answer will come. When you follow through with that, you ultimately carry on in an intentional state. And if you recognize you have become disconnected, just follow the same process—simply reconnect by asking yourself: *What is my intention? What are my outcomes and my purpose*? Then, you can follow those specific directions, rather than following other people's directions and being somebody who lives their life in a reactive state.

STAYING CONNECTED TO THE UNIVERSAL ENERGY

We know that we're part of the universe, and we know some about the planets operating in the solar system. But that's as far as our collective knowledge goes. The truth is there's potentially an infinite universe of energy we're part of and that's available to us. We can be an active part of this universal energy—receiving, facilitating, harnessing, and utilizing all the energy that exists—instead of being whipped around by it. We feel life in a completely different way when we collaborate with it.

Just like a bike has wheels that propel it forward, the motion is going forward through life. All the energy is moving forward because you direct it that way. The opposite would be to feel like life and the world is happening *to* you, as many people do.

When you think about the cycles and patterns swirling through the universe, we are all part of a matrix. There's so much energy that's in motion, and if we don't recognize that and we're disconnected from ourselves, we ultimately feel like life is beating us up.

We've all been exposed to notions like *life is hard* and *nothing good comes easy*. We almost expect that life is supposed to be an uphill battle. But what if, in fact, we're supposed to be supported as part of everything that's in the world? What if our job is simply to be connected to our Selves and stay true to our Selves (which it is)? That's why this Commitment is so foundational. Without it, people have a lot of confusion and feel that life is full of scarcity and without purpose. And that's a very frightening way to live.

We as humans can feel very alone in the world, even though it's full of everything. The universe is really ours, and we belong to the universe. We are all one process going on with many different components, animals, and people. When you build a relationship with your Self, it allows you to be connected to the vastness—and the closeness—of these systems and to know that they are part of us and we are all part of the same systems that are moving forward. We, and the world, cycle through days and nights, seasons, and years.

COMMITMENTS QUESTION: What do I believe about the world—do I think that the universe has my back?

Our conditioning has programmed us to see reality in a certain way, in the framework that our parents, relatives, friends, and communities have. Even something like death is simply a concept, this idea that once we die, we are gone. But being connected to our Selves allows us to recognize that we are in a boundless energetic field where everything is occurring—one that we likely do not leave simply because we've left our human body.

As I see it, there is no end to the cycle. When we pass away, that energy is going somewhere else. This is actually quite congruent with religion as well as agnosticism. Whether you believe in heaven and hell, reincarnation, or just something after this life, it's all about energy moving on. Or, if you believe we simply return to the earth, that's an energy shift too. I really think of this as the collective conscious and unconscious, where all of this energy is running through everything. Even if something looks like it's not part of this energy, it's simply part of a cycle. Some cycles are short, and others are long.

So there's no reason to fear death. It is not "the end." It is merely the next step in the journey. What that energetic journey entails, we won't know until we get there.

Humans have essentially been in a lot of intentional cycles. Throughout history, we've been at our finest and highest capacity when we've been connected to ourselves and to our outcomes, and we have triumphed by staying focused on those outcomes. For example, think of the pyramids—manmade marvels that we could say don't even make sense for the capacity we believe humans had at that time. Similarly, the Duomo in Florence, Italy: think of the architect and the crafters of the Duomo and all of the generations of people who created that structure and were following their intentions. That's what people are capable of when they follow the first Commitment to stay connected to themselves.

The ability to stay connected to your intentions and all of the intelligence that is available to us allows humans to be focused on the contributions that they are here to do. Certain people are here to construct architectural plans, and others are here to fulfill those architectural plans, one tile or brick at a time. Neither purpose is any less noble or grand than the other. When all of us connect to our internal navigation system, that provides directions for what it is we are here to do. But the reality is that staying connected to your outcomes through your internal navigation system can only come through the process of staying connected to your Self.

It's no secret that some people can be emotionally more sensitive than others. While some people have a narrower field of perception for feelings, others seem to be better able to feel everything that is going on in the environment. This can be thought of as negative—*"Quit being so sensitive"*—but it can actually be a superpower, granting a top-level conscious awareness. This sensitivity is actually a way of being connected without recognizing that you're connected. But that's how it can also negatively impact people, chronically conditioning them, putting them on sensory overload, and creating cycles that are not intentional.

There's a range of emotional sensitivity. Emotionally sensitive people may believe they are attuned to their surroundings, but they typically are not aware of most of the things in the environment that are impacting them.

When emotionally sensitive people are told there's something wrong with them, that they are wrong for having feelings, this begins to create patterns of stress, confusion, and difficulty. But that's why it's so important for them to learn that we are in fact connected with everything—in fact, there's nothing wrong with them.

If you fall in the category of being emotionally sensitive, knowing that we are all interconnected, you can track and monitor yourself. This is a game-changer because you know if you're in a connected, intentional state or if you feel disconnected—and that disconnection is actually you being impacted by everything you're already connected to, without realizing it.

This is so powerful in being able to know, are you in a reaction pattern, or are you in an intention pattern? Are you focused on your outcomes or being impacted by your reactions? This is essential for every person's life, but perhaps even more critical for the emotionally sensitive among us.

THE ROLE OF TECHNOLOGY

Technology brings about an even greater responsibility to commit to this core Commitment to stay connected to your Self and to tune into your internal navigation system so you aren't thrown off of your intentions or wallowing in reactions.

Becoming connected to your Self is about recognizing every single thing that is going on and being able to assess it. As we are in this era where everybody is texting and emailing, there are continuous cycles of energy going from person to person through all of these technological platforms—it's a whole new age of reactions and intentions that are being facilitated in this way. And while people have been able to fulfill incredible outcomes and innovations that much more quickly, they have also never been more reactive because there's a greater amount of energetic motion. Think of news articles touting the reactions of the Twitterverse within minutes or hours of an event occurring.

It's not surprising that in this time of great technological advancement, humankind is also going through an incredibly difficult emotional cycle of adjustment: as a collective, as individuals, and as different pockets of society. Never before has there been more anxiety, more depression, and more of every single kind of emotional difficulty. Reactive patterns can also include anger, procrastinating, eating, drinking, gambling, shopping, and the list goes on.

COMMITMENTS QUESTIONS: When I think of a more evolved world, what does that look like? How might I uniquely contribute to that?

As you think of this powerful Commitment to your Self, truly recognize that you're capable of taking all the conditioning that has happened to you and using your creative capacity to shape your life. In this way you can be in the flow of life, rather than being separate and being in scarcity and strain. You can pass on those difficulties and the stories that go along with them—*Life/this job/marriage/etc. is supposed to be hard*—that create the opposite of what humans are here to do, which is to evolve society to a more elevated place throughout each of our lifetimes. And when we become clear about this, ultimately our specific purpose is known to us.

When we live in purpose, all things that we do become purposeful, meaningful, and fulfilling. And this makes us people who are not only changing the world, but people who are here to create the very world that we want to exist. And this puts all humans into the ability to create whatever they are here to create and desire, regardless of their previous circumstances and their previous conditioning.

I invite you to apply this Core Commitment of staying connected to your Self to every single moment that you can, and to reconnect over and over again throughout your lifetime, and to support others around you to do the same.

First and foremost, stay connected to your Self. As Shakespeare wrote in *Hamlet*, "to thine own self be true." This first foundational Core Commitment to your Self will provide you with the emotional foundation that you need to add in the additional Core Commitments.

CHAPTER 3

Commitment Two

*Be Intentional, Accurate, and Factual in
Your Speech with Yourself and Others*

To ADD TO OUR PRIMARY GOAL—WHICH IS TO BE
connected to our Selves—we're also here to recondition ourselves and our communication process.
We want to shape it into a very productive rhythm
and pattern so that we are efficient, healthy, vibrant,
happy, and wealthy—all the things everybody aspires
to, but often struggles to achieve.

The second Commitment sets you up for a big
emotional transformation: the commitment to
communicate with intentionality, accuracy, and
factuality. While those are related, they are all important in their own right.

Let's break each of them down:

- *Intentionality:* Having what you intend match what you are communicating. For example, if you intend to comfort a friend who is going through a hard time, you express your concern, make eye contact, and offer a hug. Being less intentional might mean you talk about other things with your friend and avoid eye contact and touching because it's uncomfortable to discuss what she's struggling with.

- *Accuracy:* Communicating clearly and positively. Many people communicate what they *don't* want, or in negative terms, which can be confusing. "I don't want to eat Chinese food for lunch" does not describe what you actually *want* to eat. Saying "I want a juicy BLT with a cup of delicious tomato soup" is a clear response—and it means you're far more likely to get what you want!

- *Factuality:* Sticking to just the facts at hand. Humans love to make up drama and stories that may be only partially true—or outright wrong. Let's say you ask your spouse a question and she replies absentmindedly. Her inattention may hurt or annoy you, but that is just your perception. The only facts are that she replied and she sounds distracted. The "why" of this is probably not as personal as it seems; you may think that she doesn't care about you, but perhaps she's thinking of her sick co-worker, making a grocery list in her head, or any number of things. Evaluating communication based on the facts helps each of us stay true to ourselves and remove unnecessary drama from our surroundings.

All of these pieces are about being in integrity with your Self. You can move from seeing yourself as sick or broken to seeing yourself as healthy and whole. Or from poor and struggling to wealthy and abundant. The transformations can be infinite.

Building on the first Commitment—to be connected to your deepest Self—this second Commitment takes it a step further to be in *integrity* with your Self. What does that mean? It includes the way you communicate to yourself and to other people.

And while we usually think of this as strictly our verbal communication, it really encompasses all our communication—our thoughts, our feelings, our body language, and the energy we put out to other people. But first and foremost, it's about how we communicate with ourselves since that is our primary relationship.

If you've ever watched RuPaul Charles's reality show *RuPaul's Drag Race*, you're probably familiar with the closing line RuPaul uses at the end of each episode: "If you can't love yourself, how in the hell are you going to love somebody else?!" And Ru is right! Let's say you're a mom, and you're trying to teach your kids to take care of themselves. You show them how to brush their teeth, comb their hair, and stick to a bedtime schedule. While that's all important, if your kids see you constantly frazzled and eating junk food, what they are also learning is not to value themselves—because you aren't taking care of your own needs. Think what a different example it is for kids to see a parent who eats well and practices self-care when they feel stressed, whether that's by taking the kids for a walk or having a few minutes to themselves. They are communicating to their kids that they are important and that the kids should treat themselves that way too.

The way we communicate, especially to ourselves, may not seem like a big deal. But this Commitment is important because we're all in this together, so the way you communicate with everyone (including yourself) has more of an impact than you may realize. Think of your next-door neighbor, your neighborhood, the town you live in, the nation you reside in, and the world at large. Be aware that there is quite honestly nothing that is not interconnected in the world. While some of this communication occurring may be positive, we also tend to cycle through communication patterns that are detrimental and destructive, which I refer to as "recycling."

This second Commitment is a powerful way to change how you process your own existence and what you can observe, as well as changing the way you process information you're aware of within yourself and others.

How do you communicate with integrity to yourself? You tell yourself what's going on, whether it's about:

- What you register in your experience

- What you are feeling—negative or positive feelings, physical sensations like a headache, etc.

Based on this, you:

- Communicate effectively about what you're going to do about it to yourself and/or others

For example, let's say you get to work and your boss is in a bad mood. You start to wonder if you did something wrong or if there are going to be layoffs. You notice that your shoulders are tense and your breath is all in your chest, not cycling down to your diaphragm. You tell yourself you will start breathing more deeply to relax yourself while you seek more information, and you ask your boss if there's anything you can help with.

COMMITMENTS QUESTIONS: How do I communicate to myself? Do I think about what's wrong and what I don't want?

It's important to note that communication is not just what we verbalize; that's just the tip of the iceberg. All different forms of communication have an impact on you and others.

Different forms of communication:

- Internal

    * Your thoughts

    * Communications from your body

    * How we visualize the future, brainstorm, and create

- External

    * Verbal communication to and from others

    * Body language

    * Written communication

    * Social media

When you commit to communicating more factually, accurately, and with intention, you may see your life in a whole new way. Instead of thinking, *I hate going to work*, you might say to yourself, *This position allows me to learn a lot each day, helps me provide for my family, and affords me some great friends.* Now, going to work doesn't feel like a chore—it's an opportunity to create more of what you want.

THE PHYSICS OF COMMUNICATION

A quick word about physics: there's a matrix of energy that is always going on. We are always in motion, and we are both cause and effect. When we are in an intentional communication process through a deeply connected relationship with ourselves and reality, we are able to see patterns of energy, emotions, relationships, and communication. We're able to register what we experience and what we want to do with that. Otherwise, we become captive to unconscious patterns of communicating.

Similar to physics, there is intention and reaction. And we are constantly in motion. At our best, we are in intentional motion. When we are in reactive motion, we are captive to patterns and largely unaware of them.

This Commitment is also an awareness that we're in a collective field. And in this collective field, so many people are struggling with negative thoughts that they don't want to have, that cause them pain and upset. In fact, this is what's going on in our society as a whole (you don't have to look any further than our current toxic political culture to see that). And we are responsible to ourselves to shift these things into intentional communication. Each of us is totally responsible for what we register and recognize so that we take it and reorganize it through our ability to communicate. This will emanate outward into everything that we are connected to—which is everything.

That's why it's important to know that we are receiving at all times—even when we're chilling on the couch watching Netflix, we are still receiving from this vast energetic field. If we want to know why we can be so affected by things—especially those of us who are emotionally sensitive—it's because we're absorbing the world around us. We are receiving communication and registering it. Communication is an active practice through the words you use and tone of voice, and how you relate to people, write to people, and present to people with your body language.

COMMITMENTS QUESTIONS: What do I want in my life? Can I practice telling myself this?

This is why it's important to build off of the first Commitment. When you are connected to your Self and the present moment, you're moving your intentions, energy, and communications in a forward direction that is clear and accurate.

We can feel helpless to change our thoughts or slow them down. Buddhists refer to this as "monkey mind," the endless, anxious, scattered chatter in our heads. When we don't know how to harness these thoughts, we keep recycling them. And they get out into the world—either in our own living room, through social media, or through any way in which people are in motion.

But know that you are creating every moment. There is a process that should be directed with intentionality, communicated in factual, clear, assertive, accurate language of what you intend and how you would like to take the power of the moment to cultivate something. This responsibility exists, whether we choose to take it on or not.

In our physics equation, every single human is creating the world and is equally as powerful in creating the opposite of what they want, whether they know it or not. What I think, write, say, and do is creating for myself and other people, and what other people do is creating for me as well. *Everything that we are doing is creating for each other, making it a complete and total world of what we all want to create.* If you create with intention, life is being created that way, and if you create out of reaction, it's being created that way too.

If you want a positive life, you need to reorganize your negative thoughts into something that will address what you're feeling negative about in a constructive way. For example, let's say you haven't found the right partner in life. Failed relationships have left you feeling bruised and like it's just not going to happen for you. If you're constantly thinking, *I have such bad luck in relationships* or *I'll never find the right person*, you'll stay stuck in that energy and may even repeat it several more times. But if you shift your thoughts along the lines of, *I've learned so much about the kind of relationship that will work for me* and *I'm making space for a person who is kind, calm, and positive in my life*, you're shifting negativity into clear, open communication.

COMMITMENTS QUESTION: What kind of energy am I putting out to others through my verbal communication, body language, and attitude?

Stress tends to arise when we feel some awareness of this matrix of energy, but it doesn't feel good. While we are paying attention, it's often in a reactive way, not an intentional one—it feels like one shoe dropped, and we're bracing ourselves for the other to fall too. And just because we can't see or hear what's going on in other places, like our neighbor's house, doesn't mean that's not part of our experience.

In a world where people are in a lot of emotional difficulty—unintentional, reactive, unclear, inaccurate, negative forms of communicating—they're in action. And this action can affect you too since we're all connected. The way you're directing your attention (with intention) out to the world really benefits not just you, but everyone else as well. We are creating the world we live in; it's much more empowering to be very clear in what you're communicating to yourself and what you're communicating to other people on all levels.

We are always in motion, and our system is always "on." Even when we sleep, our bodies are digesting food, replenishing energy stores, and our minds are actively dreaming. Our system is designed for us to go forward, to deal with the now, not the past. And the systems in the body communicate with each other, as well. For example, when you're under acute stress, your body goes into fight-or-flight mode. The body releases hormones, which activate your sympathetic nervous system. Your heart rate increases, muscles tighten, and breath shortens. The body's instructions are sequenced toward an outcome, which is keeping you safe from perceived danger.

These functions of the body run parallel to us too. Our bodies are automated to do things so we don't have to think about them, like a heart beating and eyes blinking. Our own Self is doing that, but our bodies are also trying to communicate with us as well.

Everything that makes up our personality, that is truly sequenced for us. But as we've discussed, we're also constantly absorbing the conditioning of our atmosphere and those around us too. The challenge is to get back to our Selves, to see what our bodies and minds are communicating to us.

Think of the power of meditation. When we connect to breathing, we connect to our Selves. This is the reality of what we're meant to be doing. Within these directions lies our navigation for our unique path in life.

That direction contains the answers to the age-old questions humans struggle with in each generation: Where do I go? What's the purpose of my life? Your internal GPS already knows about you because it's coded for you. It *is* you. You need to communicate with yourself deeply, receiving the communication and giving that communication back to yourself so that it's clear the message is between you and you—versus you and everyone else.

You can probably think back to some point in your life when you were faced with a choice, and your internal navigation was telling you one thing, but your loved ones or society or your grade-school teacher was telling you to do the opposite. It could be something as simple as whether or not to take a day off from work, or something as major as who you married. If you decided to follow the advice of other people instead of your own, you probably regret the decision or at least wonder what would have happened if you'd chosen to follow your own inner wisdom.

When we communicate to ourselves with integrity, it elevates our frequency—not just with ourselves, but with other people. It will raise the frequency of those we're in close proximity with too. Conversely, we don't even have to be in the same room as someone to impact them with our frequency. If you're in your bedroom thinking negative thoughts over and over, this builds up a negative frequency, and that frequency is going out. So your spouse, even if he's in the basement, will be impacted by this as well.

When we're in conversation, we don't always have to verbalize negative thoughts for another person to be aware of them. If your spouse asks how your day was and you say, "Fine!" but glare at him and sound annoyed, your spouse knows that you are not fine at all. Although we're conditioned to communicate verbally, we aren't conditioned to pay attention to how we communicate overall—our energy and motion, which are just as impactful, if not more so.

Think of yourself reading this book, practicing The Commitments, and the positive impact it has on you and your immediate circle of people. Then think of all the other people reading this book, sharing it, and exuding it. The results are truly amazing. And the same thing goes if people are sharing the worst of the worst with themselves, talking all the time about what's wrong or painful. There's a paradigm shift needed, but the opportunity also is great.

We're here to live out our potential and create the potential of this world that we live in. The beauty of these Commitments is that they are not just for people who have been born in wealth and stability. *The Commitments work for anyone in any situation, from the worst impoverished conditioning, for people at any stage of life, from young to very old.* If enough people practice The Commitments, it leads to a major societal upgrade, shifting us from a world of perceived lack and struggle to one where there is plenty for everyone. We can create the world we want to create together. It is a collaboration and a partnership.

It's not a coincidence that most of the major religions have the concept of heaven and hell. Heaven is this utopia that we can actually achieve on Earth by making these upgrades, just as hell is the pain and struggle we already see here in the world. And ultimately when it is upgraded, the suffering paradigm will shift because everyone will be connected to themselves, connected to life itself, and connected to each other. Instead of being affected by each other, we'll be able to share and love and prosper.

It is human nature to tell stories, and to be compelling, stories need drama. We unwittingly do this in our own lives—we create villains and victims and the need for ourselves to be overly heroic, which is exhausting. But in order to have a true happy ending, we need to tell ourselves the truth.

If you're waiting for a friend and they are late, you may spin this a lot of ways as you sit by yourself: *she hesitated when I invited her to lunch; maybe she's not coming.* Or, *We're drifting apart.* Or, *She's upset about what I said the last time we got together.* But all of these are simply interpretations; the only factual read on this event is to say to yourself, *She's running late.* None of these other interpretations are true, at least until she arrives and you find out more. In the meantime, they can cause you pain and suffering.

Another tip: if you're using "never" or "always," you're not being factual. As in, *She's always so inconsiderate.*

We continuously want to be fact-checking because if we tell ourselves these stories and don't check them for accuracy, we're operating in alternative facts—and therefore an alternative reality. This makes it very hard to create the reality that we want. If we ask ourselves the simple question—*how does that benefit me to believe something that is not factual?* —the answer is inevitably that it's not.

When you realize that you're in a dramatized, negative narrative, make a shift. Give yourself permission only to speak factually and intentionally.

What might these positive communications be about? They could be about improving your home or the food you're buying to make healthy meals. Or about building a new project, writing a book, or teaching your children. These are all about the things you do, guiding you to the outcomes you want. And you want to start communicating them as outcomes, not just fragments of something.

We often think in terms of what someone is not doing, like, *I can't believe he hasn't taken out the trash yet.* But the truth is that the universe isn't designed to understand the negative; *what somebody is not doing*

isn't communicating something the universe can work
with. Instead, it's important to communicate what is.
My husband is driving to the store.

Pay attention to how you talk to yourself too. The
way you talk about yourself is the way you talk about
everybody, even if it's indirect. If you think to yourself, *I'm fat, and I hate the way I look,* this self-loath-
ing will transfer to how you speak to other people and
the kind of frequency you carry in the world, even if
you think it doesn't.

Have you ever heard of Abraham Maslow? Or
Maslow's hierarchy of needs? If you haven't, his
theory is something that you know intuitively.
The idea is that you need to meet your most basic
needs before you can address other needs. Anyone
who's been a new parent knows about operating
in "survival mode." When you're dealing with a
newborn, just taking a shower and getting choppy
amounts of sleep are all the self-care you can muster.
Higher-up needs like socializing with friends or
having time for yourself go out the window for a
while since you are focused completely on the needs
of your baby and your basic survival in order to care
for that child.

According to Maslow, there are five levels of human needs, and before you can attend to the "higher up" needs, you must address the lower ones. The most basic needs are physiological, followed by safety, love and belonging, esteem, and finally, self-actualization.

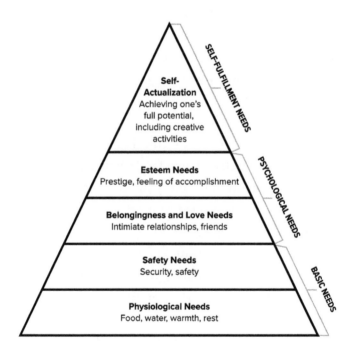

Maslow's hierarchy of needs.[2]

---

2 Dr. Saul McLeod, "Maslow's Hierarchy of Needs," Simply Psychology, December 29, 2020, https://www.simplypsychology.org/maslow.html.

The Commitments are how we address all of these needs and reach self-actualization.

Wherever you're at, whatever is going on, you build on it. You tell yourself the truth. And you communicate the facts of all that you have available to you.

THE MYTH OF SCARCITY

Observe the difference between these ways of describing the same scenario:

- "We're missing/we're out of/we don't have milk. What else are we out of?"

- "We have plenty of food for the week. I'm also going to get milk. Would you like to add to the list?"

The first example talks about lack; the second talks about abundance. This is the way that we were intended to be: to be able to recognize what is, and wherever we are conditioned to recognize what isn't, to instead acknowledge what we will create more of.

A lot of news headlines, and even a lot of everyday conversations, focus on scarcity. What people don't have, what isn't working, and what's bad. But if you look at overarching reality, scarcity is a myth. Even in first-world countries, we have people who don't know where their next meal is coming from, despite the fact that 30–40 percent of the US food supply goes to waste.[3] There are people who believe that if something good happens to another person, it means that it's somehow been taken away from them: a job promotion, finding the right partner, or taking an amazing vacation. None of this is true—we are free to create our own opportunities, and there is enough for everyone. In fact, it's limitless.

The good news is that when you make this paradigm shift from unproductive, negative language to factual, intentional language, there are no barriers to where you can go. And everyone wants to be limitless; being limited feels terrible. Whether you come from complete poverty or from more material wealth, this is available to you.

---

3 "Food Loss and Waste," US Food & Drug Administration, accessed December 20, 2020, https://www.fda.gov/food/consumers/food-loss-and-waste.

COMMITMENTS QUESTIONS: What do I want to create more of in my life? Can I practice building abundance?

When somebody thinks there isn't enough of something, then there isn't. This is all negative, lower-frequency thinking, which brings about scarcity and suffering. Perhaps you've had a friend who loved to complain about his job, but he didn't take any steps to make his job more bearable or find a new one. The truth is people can get addicted to complaining. It gives them plenty of other people to commiserate with!

Conversely, when very wealthy people keep talking to each other about more wealth-building, they gain more; they see opportunity. They see the limitlessness of it, and they keep building. But this positive focus works even when someone doesn't have a lot of money. If you're counting your pennies, you're still counting. You're focusing on how you can build more abundance, which leads you to self-actualize.

It isn't just people in material poverty who feel scarcity. The world conditions the wealthiest people into emotional poverty too, where they feel a scarcity that doesn't exist—instead of sharing more of their abundance, they feel they must keep all of their wealth.

The scarcity story is one we've believed generation after generation. It keeps those with less wealth stuck in the mentality that they will never have enough, and for those who do have wealth, it keeps them cultivating resources for fear that at any moment, those resources could be gone because the world is so chaotic and scarce. And as long as that communication is operating in any one of us, it is operating in every one of us, and it will continue.

WHY WE GET WHAT WE DON'T WANT

When a member of my team does a consultation conversation with a new client or potential client, we talk about what it is they want. And nine times out of ten, people will answer four to five things that they know they *don't* want. This is one of the most significant and detrimental communication issues—people know so much of what they don't want. That's what they're walking around with and talking about. But ironically, knowing what we don't want is the surest way to create more of it because where we put our attention grows. We can *grow* scarcity. Even though that may sound like a paradox, that's how powerful we are.

When we communicate intentionally with ourselves, it means we want to operate at our highest Self. And therefore, we're communicating in the positive, assertive form. We speak about what we want to be, where we're going, and what we're creating. This keeps us moving forward in our intentions, instead of backward into reactive patterns that slow our progress.

You are creating every moment. This is a process that should be directed with intentionality and communicated in factual, clear, assertive, accurate language of what you intend and how you would like to take the power of the moment and cultivate something.

At the end of someone's life, we often talk about the life they led. But for many people, it was the life they *experienced*, or maybe they lived, but it wasn't necessarily the life that they led. Where they were just living instead of leading, they likely had some mixed results and a lot of pain and suffering. But this Commitment is a shift into a completely different existence. This is a shift into an elevated state of being, leading, and doing everything in this higher-frequency realm throughout life.

With everything you recognize that you don't want, I invite you to shift this communication and replace it with what you *do* want, what you *do* intend. We'll talk about this even more in the next Commitment.

CHAPTER 4

Commitment Three

*Choose Your Intentions, and Focus on
Your Outcomes Over Your Feelings*

BUILDING OFF OF THE PREVIOUS COMMITMENTS,
the third Commitment is about getting very clear and
focusing on what you want to create—no matter what
life throws your way. It's to choose your intentions
and then to focus on your outcomes, even when difficult, conditioned feelings come up (as they will).

This concept can be tricky because in some circles we
are taught to ignore our feelings, and in others, we are
taught to be led exclusively by our feelings. Either of
these can cause pain and suffering. And it's important to remember that what you think of as "your
feelings" may not exactly be yours—they may just be

a set of conditioned reactions that you've learned. That's why, as you learned in Commitment One, you constantly want to check in with your Self and see if you're in a reaction or an intention.

For example, let's say your mother didn't talk about her feelings when you were growing up. She stuffed down her emotions, but they would bubble up anyway in the form of angry shouting or drinking to numb herself. So now as an adult you have trouble expressing emotion, not just because you didn't have a good example of how to do so, but because you associate it with volatility. But if you check in with yourself when you get this urge to clam up, you can realize what's happening and gently override it, knowing that you have the right to express yourself in a productive way.

When you ask yourself, *What is my intention?*, what you really are asking is, *What are the outcomes that I want to create, and what are the incomes that I'm wanting?* Your outcomes and incomes are a result of what you believe, what you perceive, what you conceive, and what you receive altogether, in each moment of your existence.

Both outcomes and incomes go under the category of our intention. So, to stay on track in life and live your potential, your main focus needs to be on your intentions—the highest level of emotion you can create. You're taking all the energy in the world and shaping it with your focus.

You may be familiar with the book *The Secret* and the law of attraction—the idea that we are attracting something all the time. In reality, I believe *you're* ***creating*** *something all the time, which means that specificity counts.*

Our purpose is to be very comfortable in our intentions and in designing the specifics of what we want, whether it's a beautiful living room, a set amount of money, the ideal partner, or anything else. But to get there, you have to know what you want and be able to mentally place yourself there before you've actually arrived.

Let's say your dream is to run in the Boston Marathon. Now, running a marathon is an achievement to begin with. You have to run over twenty-six miles! That requires getting in shape, training, and discipline. Everyone knows that you can't just show up on race day and lace up your sneakers; you need time to work your way up to this level of endurance. On top of that, if you're going to run in a highly competitive race like the Boston Marathon, you have to first qualify for it by doing other marathons and complete them in a set amount of time based on your age and gender.

But before all that, you have to see yourself as healthy—as someone who is capable and deserving of achieving such a big milestone. You need to be able to tell yourself, "I'm a runner," and believe it. When you do so, it can help you start to make those small changes you need to; you start stretching, drinking more water, picking out a running outfit, and jogging around the block.

In life, you can either be in despair and depression, or you can be in enthusiastic intention and already living out your vision as you imagine it, feeling it into the future and specific in how you design it. Which sounds better to you?

People tend to think that it takes a huge amount of time to create something they want, but really, *it's more about the amount of time that you spend in your* **intentions.** Quite honestly, if you're serious about your intentions, you just don't have time to be constantly in reaction, thinking about what isn't and what you don't have—because the more you do and the more you get used to living there, the more you're generating that reality. And the more you get used to it—even though you don't want it—the more you believe it, making it that much harder to recondition yourself.

Instead, when we stay in intention, we stay open to the intelligence we are receiving from everything in the universe. Some refer to this as God, or Spirit, or simply universe. It's really just understanding that when we ask ourselves what our intention is, we are receiving that intention as much as we are creating with it.

COMMITMENTS QUESTIONS: What are my intentions? How specific can I get about them?

Let's look at a common goal: making money. If you want to make $100 million, you can't just think about it for five seconds and expect it to manifest. All of your other conditioning is firing off the rest of the time. But if you stay with your intention over and over—no matter what else pops up, what you absorb from others, what you come across on social media, and what counter-conditioning to your intention comes up—you can reach your goal. *Your ability to be completely, consistently connected to your specific outcomes is the secret to creating them.*

The specifics of what we want are important. If you ask yourself your intention and you think, *I want to be healthy,* that's a start. But then, keep asking yourself, *What is the rest of my intention?* Does healthy to you mean having bright white teeth, exercising with a friend, or becoming a vegan? The specifics are fundamentally important. This goes for everything, including our relationships.

When I ask clients what they want, it's interesting to witness people get very uncomfortable stating their intentions, especially when it comes to money. This is a telltale sign of their reactivity and their conditioning. But it's also the main thing keeping them from having exactly what they want because you not only need to be able to choose your intentions with specificity, but to live in them repeatedly. As you put your focus on intention, it allows you to feel more and more comfortable with it so that it's easy for you to create it—because it becomes who you are. It becomes conditioned into your being, and it replaces all of the conditioning that is counter to what you really want.

Reorganizing all of our reactivity into our intentions isn't just something we do on an individual level. It's also how we shift collectively too. Think about the power of voting and how much that has altered us collectively over the last several years.

Because we're all in this together, we can be at the effect of what someone else might be creating without even being connected to it. They might be creating something reactive, unproductive, or even destructive, so it's all the more important that we counter all of that by being connected to our intentions so that they materialize. And when we do that, we not only do that for ourselves; we end up doing that for everyone.

Let's face it: life is distracting. We are constantly being pulled in different directions, interrupted, and given new information that can throw us off all the time.

Think of when you watch a movie—you are sitting passively, watching the images on the screen. You know the story isn't real, but either consciously or subconsciously, you're engaged and taking in certain messages. These messages are becoming part of your conditioning.

Everybody's yard, everybody's car, every commercial that you watch on TV, every message that you see on social media, every brand, and every single thing in the environment is a piece of stimuli that is either going to unconsciously impact you, or you are going to consciously choose your intentional response to it. And you'll either choose to incorporate those references, or you'll filter out those references and make choices accordingly. Either way, there's a process of discernment going on. We're always processing, whether we're aware of it or not. This can be passive and unintentional, or we can use The Commitments to do this intentionally.

If we're not in intention, it's easy to get pulled into other peoples' agendas. *A lot of suffering comes from prioritizing our reactions to other people as opposed to staying with our intentions.*

Let's say your intention is to exercise five days a week. You've found an exercise class you like and gotten into a rhythm of going once you get off of work. But then, life starts to butt in: your husband wants to eat new dinners that take a lot more time to cook, and your friend is going through a breakup and wants to meet up for happy hours. Suddenly, it's a struggle to stick to your intentions. You decide your exercise goal is going to have to be put on hold indefinitely. As you meet others' needs instead of your own, you become increasingly resentful.

Well, I'm here to tell you that in many cases, you can prioritize your intentions over others' feelings. I know this may sound controversial, but understand that what any given person is "feeling" at any given time is not necessarily who they are. It can just be a conditioned response. Your husband thinks he can't cook, but in reality he is capable of cooking dinner a few nights if he wants to try new recipes, and your friend can meet you for lunch (so she skips the booze too). When you stick with your intentions, you're able to be a better partner and friend, so it actually helps you to help others as well.

COMMITMENTS QUESTION: How often do I prioritize others' intentions over my own?

How do you tell the difference between intuition and just a feeling? What's the difference between a conditioned reaction and an intuitive response? One hint: if you feel stress (which is often a reaction), then you're in a conditioned response to something that is operating out of a belief. That's the importance of knowing specifically what you want.

This can be complicated because collectively, we're told to be in connection with our feelings. It's not a bad thing to be aware of your feelings, but *what you really need to be in connection with is your navigation system.* As we talked about in the previous Commitments, this is different from your feelings. We are taught by society to follow a prescriptive path for life, so following your intuition can seem abnormal and scary.

This isn't to say that you can never change course or alter some of your intentions. If your son gets sick, your exercise routine can shift to being a YouTube video you do at home until he gets better. Your feelings are still valid and important, but this is more about not letting them run roughshod over your intentions.

People get confused about concepts like karma. What's more accurate to say is that we exist in *energy*, and this energy is always in motion. We need to give that moving energy a direction. When we are clear on our intentions, that starts to direct the energy in a forward momentum—a creative, inspired, intelligent direction.

We're all walking around with a self-concept that is all of our beliefs piled up together. You believe yourself to be that person, rather than a compilation of mostly unconscious and some conscious beliefs.

There are countless belief systems. For example, there's the military belief system, and within that there are the Army, Navy, Air Force, and Marines belief systems. Scientology is a belief system, and so is Weight Watchers. Even if we don't know these belief systems personally or subscribe to them, they are still swirling around. Holidays are a belief system, whether we choose to celebrate them or not. These beliefs are automated conditioning, driving our lives without us knowing. Some of them we're aware of, and much of them we are not. We are unconsciously reacting and being propelled in directions that may not align with our intentions.

In any situation, we need to ask ourselves, *What are my intentions?* It could be to be healthy, to be happy, to be vibrant, to be free, to have $10 million in your bank account. *There are no actual limitations; it's actually always emotional limitations.* When you understand this, it holds the key to your life changing: asking yourself, *What are my intentions?* and choosing those.

I had a client, Dan, who had a belief that someone in his family always had to be sick. His worldview was that no matter how good life can be, there was always something dragging him down. Somebody had to be sick or struggling, and that made life normal. If someone wasn't sick around him, Dan became sick in order to normalize the situation to his beliefs—even though he had no idea he was doing this to himself. This story he made up wasn't factual; it was an interpretation. Having that interpretation stored, and then ultimately having that become a reference point, created a bias for the next moment. Dan picked these beliefs up from his mother, who created these emotionally driven illnesses, and likely she picked that up from family members before her.

This is just one example among many beliefs that are inaccurate. They don't actually make any sense, but if

we believe them, they only limit us more. Such conditioned beliefs require us even more to choose our
intentions to override them.

When I have a client with a limiting belief, I often ask,
How does it benefit you to believe this? And the answer
is always that it doesn't.

When you ask yourself, *What is my intention?* and you
get answers, this is the true Self, the purposeful Self
talking. That is the Self that is doing everything it can
to be fully expressed and set free from the prison of
conditioned, limiting, unconscious beliefs that are
not factual. All of these thoughts, all of these beliefs,
and all of these emotions are part of a psychological
infrastructure that was created by those who came
before us.

The great news about being a person is that we get to
choose. We get to choose our intention, our outcomes,
and our incomes, rather than being at the mercy
of whatever absorbed beliefs and conditioning can
decide for us without our knowledge or permission.

When we choose our intentions, we create new
emotional cycles, intentional cycles that continue on

and get just as internalized and ingrained as the old cycles. They become what we believe in, what we are automated to experience and receive. And that's a very powerful capacity that we have to keep creating the Self, to keep creating these emotional structures that serve us. It's an active, creative process. *Every single person—regardless of their current conditioning and their current conditions—has this powerful, creative, emotional capacity.* And these Core Commitments are the most effective, easiest, efficient, and productive way to make these changes.

CHANGING BELIEFS TO WORK FOR US

Here is another example: a different client of mine, Erik, found out that a dear friend in his life passed away. Many people believe when someone's body shuts down and passes on, you lose that person. But Erik chose to celebrate life more. He recognized that he could go into the conditioned reaction of grief, sadness, despair, and loss. But he was connected to himself and aware that these are automated stories about what happens when someone dies.

By following these Commitments, recognizing his reaction, and then choosing his intention, Erik was able to quite swiftly make a shift to celebrate his connection with his close friend because it brought so much into his life and allowed him to become all of himself. As Erik asked himself the intentions question over and over, he found the answer ultimately was to write something very beautiful about this person. He decided to recognize all the ways he wanted to take the friend's life and legacy and move it forward through his own life, family, and company. Erik was receiving the next piece of his friend's influence in his life.

Erik continued to choose his intentions over and over, rather than succumb to belief structures that he didn't even want to believe in.

On a personal note, some of the most incredible outcomes and incomes I've ever created came as a result of me transforming the most excruciatingly painful emotions I could ever imagine a person feeling and using every one of The Commitments to reshape the conditioned patterns of shock, trauma, heartbreak, and loss into the most amazing experiences of empowerment and creativity. At times in my life where I could've *checked out* of life as way to stop the pain, I did the opposite, and I used these Core Commitments of The Method to *check in* with my Self so I could turn those moments of pain into moments of profound purpose, prosperity, and peace for myself and others.

One such time for me was when my father passed away, as I watched the conditioned reactions of grief and loss well up inside of me. But instead of letting these be the definitive experience I had of my father's passing, I used my intentions to instead make the experience ultimately beneficial for me.

The reality is that the avoidance of these patterns is a way that we negate how powerful we are to use emotions for our optimal creativity. *It's the avoidance of emotions that creates the greatest pain, while the harnessing of them is where all of our power lies.* If we attempt to run from the power that is there, it will overpower us because all of the energy needs direction or it creates chaos. When you give all of this emotional energy a direction, you get to experience just how powerful of a creator you really are.

Many people struggle with relationships, and this is often because they aren't 100 percent clear about the life they want. Maybe you think, *I just want a nice partner.* But you need to be specific about what that means to you. Think about the partnership itself, how you want to experience life, what your priorities are, what you're wanting to create together as a couple, the life that you envision, the values that you have, and when things are created (such as if and when to have kids). Most people are far too narrow about what they consider in a partner—they think about physical attributes, common interests, or employment. Think not just about "you" or "this other person," but about "we" and what that will look like.

A lot of relationships are formed out of reaction, meaning you will have mixed results at best. Reactions are, in a way, choosing you, instead of you choosing your intentions. Also, because reactions can be so powerful, you can end up with people who are recycling the same patterns that you've had in your family for generations. Think of the abused child who goes on to marry an abusive spouse, even though they don't want to. Because of conditioning, people can end up with relationships that are very dissatisfying, and this is such an area of confusion for them. But it actually isn't all that complex when you understand the emotional science going on.

The reaction you have to others isn't necessarily from something deep within yourself; it can be a familiar pattern of reactivity to particular people because their patterns fit in with the patterns that you're conditioned for. This is often the reason someone is attracted to another person because they are in an experience of being captivated by patterns and cycles. That's why some people often repeat the same struggles and issues in relationships over and over throughout their life, and these same dysfunctions can even happen over and over through the generations of a family.

This doesn't just apply to romantic relationships, but to friendships as well. The cycles with other people that we are drawn into are sometimes productive and intentional, but others are reactive, unintentional things. Reactive relationships can appear good on the surface, but as time goes on, cracks start to show. And these patterns just keep recycling themselves. That's why it's so important to be connected to your Self and intentional as you choose who to partner up with in various relationships.

COMMITMENTS QUESTIONS: Do my partner and I share the same intentions? Or, if I'm single, am I clear on the life I want to have with a partner?

Romantic love is often touted as the highest, most elevated feeling people can experience in life. But love is actually one of the most destructive emotions that people can feel if it is simply a conditioned response.

I'll give you a personal example: When I was younger, I had an idea of what I wanted in a relationship, but I wasn't fully connected to my intuition. I met a man—we'll call him Mr. Charming—while I was in high school. The relationship was as dysfunctional and tumultuous as it gets, and yet my reaction to him felt like being in love. I ended up marrying him at age twenty-one, even though my navigation system was telling me that Mr. Charming was not actually my ideal.

Had I been able to be deeply connected to myself, I would have considered: *This is the life that I want. This is the relationship that I want. This is how this relationship works. This is what I want it to feel like, look like, be like, and this is what I want it to do in the world. This is what I want us to create together.*

If I'd been able to envision that life and follow my intentions instead of ignoring them, I would have been able to sift through my feelings that I loved Mr. Charming, which was really code for, *I'm attracted to him*. Really, I was in a cycle with this man that was very much the cycle of my family system, the relationship dynamics and patterns that were playing themselves out.

In my family, people were very attractive and charming, but also extremely reactive, caught in dysfunctional cycles. And my husband fit right into these patterns. Had I been able to focus on the outcomes I wanted instead of my feelings—which, more accurately, were conditioned reactions—I would have realized the marriage did not align with my intentions. Quite honestly, it would have been fairly easy to recognize that I was captive in a cycle, not genuinely in love.

I got divorced from Mr. Charming, and then I was married and divorced again. Besides me not being in intention, this pattern of conduct was created and passed down in my family. Just like my father and two generations before him, I was in a pattern of having multiple marriages. I might as well have been a puppet on a string following all of those dynamics.

These relationships were not what I intended and ended up being stressful and disappointing. In both cases, my husbands and I were not going for the same types of intentions, so the relationships were ultimately not compatible.

No matter how good a relationship may look on paper, if you're not intending a majority of things that you are here to create together, then a relationship will be in conflict. The flip side of this is that when you follow your intuition and know what life you're here to create, you're very clear about whether people fit in with that and if you are trying to create the same life together.

When you're creating a life with someone else, the specifics of that life need to be completely aligned. Now, it's normal not to be in perfect agreement—this is where you can co-create some beautiful variety that works for both people.

If you're not trying to "go to" the same place as your partner, your relationship will have chaos. It's simply physics—you can't be moving forward toward multiple places. If you have different intentions, then no matter how much you care for the other person, you'll be working against each other. There has to be a shared vision and shared intentions that work for both of you.

And if a relationship is out of alignment, a person will be reacting to that because the power of our navigation system is that it does everything it can to propel us toward our purpose. And it will keep pointing us to where we are out of alignment with what we want. Ultimately what happens is people end up blaming this on each other or blaming it on themselves. It's basically like a war with your own Self and the person for whom you have feelings. This is why you need to be able to examine for yourself the difference between a reaction of any kind—including attraction—to know what your intentions are and to map your life to those intentions.

Let's say you meet a wonderful woman who is bright, funny, and attractive. You love doing things together, and she's nice to all your friends. But as the relationship progresses, you find out that she has a bad relationship with her mother and her siblings. You're very close with your family, and she has little interest in meeting them, much less getting to know them. Intuitively, you know that this relationship isn't going to work because your family intentions are out of alignment.

The reality is that no matter how much someone may care about another person, people are here to live a specific purpose, and their lives are meant to take a particular path guided by their internal navigation system. This tells you the life you're here to create, what you're here to do and contribute, and the specific timelines of it. This information is available and accessible to you when you create an intentional relationship with yourself.

I realize that this sounds very unromantic. Everyone wants to get hit by that lightning bolt of love and feel an intense attraction. And for many people, because they are not living their purpose and potential, this is often their only experience of being fully alive. It gets idealized as the ultimate human experience, which it can be. But for some people, it can also be the greatest torture of their entire existence.

COMMITMENTS QUESTIONS: What do I believe about pain, chaos, and suffering? Am I open to practicing The Commitments and to the idea that life can be pleasurable and focused?

Commitment Three is the most enjoyable of the Commitments. It can be even more enjoyable than being in love. Intention creates an ease, a flow, and a relaxed level of being that allows you to be choosing your experiences, including choosing how much you feel of any other emotion. You can even choose how being in love feels, as the typical, reactive way of it can be too intense. When it doesn't have intentions shaping it, love can feel very painful inside. But with intention, you get to feel love in a way that is expansive, not explosive or destructive.

Love and fear exist on the same spectrum, on opposite ends. These are the basic emotions driving people. *In my estimation, intention is actually the highest emotion humans can have.* Intention is the highest level of frequency, and the highest form of existence, that we can operate from. That's because intention takes all energy, all the different qualities of emotion, all their flavors, and actually organizes them. Not only with the intentions as you recognize them, but the moment that you do, love becomes its most powerful form and you become its most powerful facilitator.

Intentionality is really the place where people feel the best. That's where you feel the most in flow, the most alive—the most grounded, relaxed, and focused. And you become what you really are meant to be, which is a collaborator with everything that exists. Intentionality allows you not only to align with evolution, but even to be ahead of it rather than behind it.

"Nature versus nurture" is often construed as one over the other. You are already made up of certain things—your nature—which includes your genetic coding, biology, and physiology. And then there's your personality—the personality your parents could already see in you as a baby. And then at the same time, your parents and other people conditioned and shaped you, both actively and passively.

What's great about The Commitments is that they offer a rebirth of shaping yourself, of conditioning and reorganizing your emotions. Imagine what it would be like if, from childhood, you had been consistently directed to ask yourself your intentions. *Imagine if your whole life, you were always connected to your Self.* And when you weren't and you were in stress, you were continually redirected to connect with your Self and to be asked what your intentions were, so that ultimately the answer would be there all the time, until eventually you didn't even have to have to ask for it. You were just conditioned for these intentions. And any moment you were struggling, your parents helped you reconnect to your Self. Isn't that amazing to think about? Well, you can do that for yourself now and for the rest of your life. And you can do it for your children too.

People can be in therapy their whole lives, and although they are trying to cope with difficult emotions, they are often actually processing the pain of their parents and grandparents, as well as their own. They are in some ways reliving it and reinforcing it in a way that supposes all of that pain was real the whole time it was happening, rather than some of it being conditioning.

While some reactions are genuine and embedded in our human circuitry for our own survival, some of your ancestor's reactions were just continually carried forward through their emotional infrastructure. The reality is, when you look at how all of those things that were occurring in the chaos and the confusion that people were in, you can start to understand that everything that was ever a reaction was a default response. This means you don't have to spend your whole life trying to understand yourself and everyone else, and it allows you to create the life that you want. You can acknowledge that there was stress and pain in the past, but it doesn't have to weigh you down now or in the future.

As an Emotional Scientist, if I know I'm going to absorb the environment anyway, then I want to actively absorb good intentions. I want to absorb empowering intentions, and intentions that align with the world that I know I want. It's all about being connected and knowing there is no lack of anything, only the perception of it that makes it peoples' experience.

When I did a TED Talk, I connected deeply with myself to consider what I wanted to share in a fifteen-minute time block. And the answer was emotional strength.[4] My intention was to create an effect in people so they had the emotional strength to shift from their reactions to their intentions. And I had many intentions that kept expanding along with it because intentions just continue to create more of themselves and create larger visions. The more you lean into them, the more

---

4   Dr. Tracy Thomas, "Emotional Strength: Dr. Tracy Thomas," filmed on October 14, 2019 at Milpitas High School, Milpitas, California, TED video, 19:20, https://www.youtube.com/watch?v=pC_bItt7o58.

you allow a chain of intentions to occur. I thought about how the audience at the TED conference would hear the talk, and then other people would be watching the video, and they would pass on the video or what they learned from it on to others, and eventually it could reach countless people. And I knew this is part of my work to create the kind of world in which I want to live.

In this society, we tend to enable reactions by adding to them and reacting even more. When a girlfriend is upset about something her boyfriend said, you may express outrage too and consider this to be empathetic. But what you're actually doing is encouraging your friend to be in those reactions over and over. And while we may give her all kinds of advice, she doesn't necessarily need our recommendations (and how many people follow through on well-meaning advice, anyway?). Maybe she is actually upset because he said something that was true, and she didn't want to hear it.

What your friend needs is to be put back smack-dab in the middle of her powerful, creative capacity in her intentions—and that is the greatest gift you could ever give her. That is the support she needs, to be redirected and focused forward into an elevated state of being. You are, in fact, emotionally training her in a way that will help her in life.

You can say to your friend, *I appreciate what you're sharing, but I'm curious—what is it that you're wanting?* Still, she may not see what's going on and what's available to her. She may not recognize that she can turn that moment into anything that she wants. You can say, *What are your priorities? What would you want to create?* From there, perhaps she can see that she really wants to address the issue her boyfriend brought up so it doesn't keep interfering in her life.

This is something that will be life-altering not just for your loved ones but for you so that you don't have to be bogged down in all kinds of reactivity in order to be close to someone, to be empathetic and in relationship with them.

As you learned in Commitment Two, our language needs to be constructive. You can help someone by getting them to focus: *What do you want? To bring in $500,000? To bring a child into the world? To bring a new friend into your life? What are the outcomes and incomes that you want? What is your vision?* And when you help people go further and further in that, their mood is immediately elevated. It gives them the road map to where they want to go, which elevates not just them but everyone.

Let's take the example of bringing in $500,000. The moment you say 500,000 dollars, you already start to feel better—because you're already in that reality. The more you live in the reality that you have $500,000, the more you experience that life already, and then the physical universe creates that. The catch is that you must stay connected to this vision, or you'll have a conflicting focus that will create chaos.

For example, if you think you want $500,000, but you're worried you won't know what to do with the money or that you'll feel more stressed once you have it, then that changes the physics around having those funds come into your life. You'll be emotionally blocking yourself into conflicting intentions—also known as *inner conflicts*.

CLEARING OUT THE CHAOS

You can put your *attention* on something, but that still doesn't mean you have *intention*. When we don't hold onto our intentions, things happen randomly and unintentionally, otherwise known as chaos. People who are living in reactive conditioning experience a lot of chaos.

In contrast, intentions can be likened to well-marked roads—there's an infrastructure of indicators, barriers, and lanes that are directing where we're supposed to go. Using the Core Commitments, you are implementing an emotional infrastructure to create what you want and where you want to go. It's like GPS; you plug in your destination, and it takes you the way to your outcome.

Accidents aren't even accidental—they are chaos and a lack of intentionality. They are due to a lack of connection, and we have the power to change that. If someone falls down on the street, it's not just an accident; the person was probably not intentional as they crossed the road. With awareness, you can recognize the obstacles you might trip over. The same concept goes for emotional science: to get where we want to go, we have to be able to look for and be aware of any emotional obstacles, hidden pieces of conditioning and beliefs, and distorted narratives. And do so in a clean, efficient, healthy way.

I don't think anyone enjoys chaos, even though a lot of people are conditioned for it. Let's say when your mom picked you up from school every day at four o'clock, she was stressed out because she'd just gotten off work, had to get you home and make dinner, and felt overwhelmed because she had no time for a break. You might find that, as an adult, you start to feel stressed every day around four o'clock, and what to make for dinner becomes this anxiety-ridden problem. It's not that you'd put yourself through this on purpose, but you're unwittingly conditioned for it.

The reality is that continually being disconnected from ourselves and only being connected to a small degree creates tiredness, exhaustion, fatigue, and irritation. *But even the idea that pain and suffering are mandatory in life is just another form of conditioning.*

When you choose intentions over and over, you're ultimately conditioning yourself for a continuous, connected state of intentionality. Instead of being connected for five seconds and dropping out of it for five hours, you can stay connected and achieve your outcomes that much faster. It is a way of being that is so lovely and almost feels like you've come "home" to a wonderful place that is sustainable, predictable, enjoyable, and relaxed.

COMMITMENTS QUESTIONS: What do I believe about pain, chaos, and suffering? Am I open to practicing The Commitments and to the idea that life can be pleasurable and focused?

Life is not meant to be as difficult as we think. It's not meant to be such terrible work. These conditions are not meant to be harsh, but our conditioning has been harsh. And the way that humans have interpreted things is overdue for a change. We must shift to the positive paradigm of what is and ask ourselves, *What are my intentions? What am I creating?* That continuous, intentional existence is something you can have until your last breath in life—that's how much power you have.

And over a period of time, you condition this response, and you never unlearn it; it is a permanent change that nobody wants to regress from. Happiness is the best conditioning for happiness. Healthiness is the best conditioning for healthiness. Creativity is the best conditioning for creativity, and wealthiness is the best conditioning for wealthiness. When you shift your conditioning and you get in this level of emotional fitness, it's like having an emotional makeover for your life. It makes life easy the way it was intended to be.

When you are not living intentionally or are in reactivity, you have things happen to you, and you are behind where it's possible to be in life. There's a terrible feeling of being conditioned for being behind. And the more you're behind, the more stress, the more reactivity, the more pressure you feel. In contrast, being in intentionality puts you in front of where you need to be, where humans need to be in evolution.

Many clients have asked me, *Will I be bored and miss the drama when I live in intention all the time?* It's no secret that we've been conditioned for drama and trauma. We create more of it and watch more of it on TV. We have yet to be conditioned for what it's like to be in continuous enjoyment of life and continuous creativity and growth. When you practice Commitment Three, you become an Emotional Scientist, and you're just continuously interested in everything that's possible.

So no, people don't get tired of creating abundance. They don't get tired of experiencing all the rewards and riches. In reality, life just keeps deepening and enriching, and it becomes more and more enjoyable and fortunate. And no, you won't miss being imprisoned by your conditioning and reactivity, and no one that you know will miss it in you.

This is the kind of energy and force that creates incredible life and incredible creations for generations forward in the future. This is what your grandchildren's grandchildren are going to get to look back on and say, *This is what my great-great-grandfather or great-great-grandmother did, and this is what they created.* And then it becomes a way of being for each family system so the next generations pick it up and take it forward. This is how we live on in the world to come.

I believe that most humans share the same intentions: to be healthy, happy, wealthy, loving, and deeply alive in purpose and potential. And they're here to channel those intentions and be a vehicle for them. Each person has their unique variation on this and how they're specifically here to carry those intentions out, which we'll talk about next in Commitment Four.

CHAPTER 5

Commitment Four

*Say and Do Only What Will
Create Your Outcomes*

WE COME NOW TO THE FINAL COMMITMENT, WHICH builds off of the previous ones and crystalizes them: to say, and do, only what will create your desired outcomes—with no exceptions. This is a very powerful Commitment that does really require all the other Commitments and the ability to keep building epic emotional strength. Every single time you move through and utilize each Commitment, this momentum builds until it becomes a flow state, where they all just work together at the speed of light. In addition, this is a level of emotional power few people ever experience in life.

Your outcomes are your biggest goals in life: the impact you want to make on the world, the people you want in your life, and how you envision success and happiness. They are the sum total of your intentions. Your intention may be to have a harmonious life, and your outcome could be to marry someone who is calm and grounded, for example.

We all know—or at least see in the media—people who seem to achieve all the goals they want. They start and build successful businesses, raise happy families, or achieve excellence in their field, whether it's sports, music, or acting, or something else highly competitive. And while their lives may not be as perfect as they seem, we at least witness that they have a powerful ability to dream and achieve what many others can't. But what they really have is the ability to focus on their outcomes and stay with them.

Well, guess what? You can do this too.

The process is to:

- Stop reacting

- Check in with your Self

- Think of your outcomes

- Choose an intention

The intention you're looking for is your highest level of intention, not just your low-level one, like, *I want my friend to feel bad because I feel bad.* Acting on your highest intention begins to give you the epic emotional strength that you need in order to start the process of saying and doing only what will create your outcomes in order to be productive, without exception.

Emotional conditioning creates behavioral conditioning, which in turn creates more emotional conditioning. For example, if your partner shuts down during a fight, you might get irritated, which causes them to shut down even more. Emotional and behavioral conditioning go hand in hand because we are dynamic human beings; what we are feeling, thinking, saying, and doing all ends up in motion together. But all of this is one system that is interconnected: mind, body, and spirit.

When we recognize that this is all one system, it starts to make life easier because we don't see these as a million separate problems to figure out. That's why The Commitments simplify all of this. Every single piece of stimuli in the atmosphere is something we are processing; when you are on a walk, you may speed up to walk around someone else, without even thinking about it. You are reacting to them.

If people go to work at a certain time, if people paint their house a certain color in a certain neighborhood, or people wear a certain kind of clothing—every single thing is a part of the matrix of influences that are going on, that we are absorbing and processing whether we are highly conscious of that or not.

COMMITMENTS QUESTIONS: Do I practice both saying and doing only what will lead me to my outcomes? Or do I get thrown off by life and my conditioning?

Say you've walked into a party and your intention is to see who's there and with whom you want to chat. But as you initially start to size up the room, somebody comes up to you and asks if you would like a drink. This can stimulate you to have a drink right away, even though you didn't intend to in that moment. And while this isn't necessarily earth-shattering, it shows you how easy it is to get thrown off your intentions.

But if you are not staying connected to yourself—knowing if you are in a reaction or an intention, being in an intention and then saying and doing only what creates the outcomes you want—then you can be taken on a ride without completely meaning to do so. And if that happens all the time, you can end up in a reactive way of being, instead of a creative one. At the party, you might end up eating three more plates of food than you planned. That way, you end up experiencing and creating things that you didn't intend.

Someone else may not have specific intentions when they go to the same party; they just want to socialize and leave at a reasonable hour because they have to work the next day. But because they don't have firm intentions and go right into reaction mode once they get there, they end up drinking too much, staying too late, and being hungover at work the following morning. And for some people, that's not just a one-time thing, but a pattern they follow day in and day out.

YOU CAN'T CHEAT THE SYSTEM

We are required to be in integrity as part of the way that manifesting outcomes happens. And this is good news because we have an emotional infrastructure called physics, or how we operate in the universe.

As we talked about in the previous chapter, physics doesn't really know the difference between "I'm not doing something" and "I'm doing something." If you talk about lack, you will create more lack. If you believe there is scarcity, you will experience more of it. If you believe there are riches everywhere, you will experience them everywhere; you will be aware of them, and they will keep generating and growing. That's how strong our powerful creative capacity is. Whatever we put our attention on will expand, period.

All the time, people intentionally or unintentionally act in a way that's counter to their desired outcomes. It's physically impossible for you to have anything else other than what you speak about, communicate about to yourself and others, and what you do.

It doesn't matter what circumstances you were born into or what you've experienced; the laws of physics only care about what you are doing in this moment and what you're going to create with it.

We all know someone who says they will do something, but they don't follow through. That's another pattern: setting an intention but then not sticking with it. Some people think they can sort of "cheat the system." They want to lose weight, but instead of changing their eating or exercise patterns, they take a diet pill. This means they are out of integrity with themselves. On some level they know this isn't the way to create lasting, healthy change, but they want a shortcut.

The universe is listening to you, but it doesn't do well with mixed messages. It just doesn't work to declare, *I want to be happy,* and then to say or think a bunch of negative things about yourself or the world. You cannot actually live in that. You have to say and do only what will create the outcomes that you've chosen and do this on a regular basis. This is how physics works, so there is no other version of you having the outcomes you want.

Many people try to stick to well-meaning goals and fail or get middling results. But in reality, people do not recognize the extent to which they are conditioned into reactive patterns. And then their whole way of speaking and acting is part of a conditioned pattern that makes it so they'll never have those outcomes the way that they want them.

COMMITMENTS QUESTION: How often is reactivity mixed up with my intentions?

The language we use to describe our outcomes is incredibly important. Let's say you weigh 180 pounds but want to weigh 120 pounds. Instead of saying, *I need to lose 60 pounds*, a more factual intention is *I'm going to utilize the energy in my body so that I weigh 120 pounds.* It's about what you *will* do, not what you won't do. *I'm going to drink water and tea; I'm going to walk for an extra ten minutes more than I usually do for the next six months.* It's not: *I'm going to cut out alcohol and creamer in coffee and stop sitting around.* You say what is going to create those outcomes. And you do those without exception. No exceptions means that the physics won't allow it—if you want certain outcomes but you act out of your reactivity instead of acting out of your intentionality, you will not have those outcomes.

If you act out of reactivity, you might have an outcome in some small degree, but you won't have it the way you really want it. Because when you're acting out of reactivity, you feel awful. If you are frustrated with your dog and you yell at her, you immediately feel bad, and your dog is upset too, even if she complies.

And the temptation to say what we don't want—*Don't talk to me that way*—is there because the conditioning for this is very strong. The conditioning in our world of what not to do, what we don't like, what we don't want—it's how parents are conditioned to talk to children: *Don't cross the street; don't splash in puddles.*

Many people want to set intentions and reach them, but they have hidden beliefs they act out that are not factual. They may say they want something but act out of another set of beliefs that will not create the outcome. So do you want someone to start doing something or stop doing something?

Commitment Four builds a lot off of Commitment Two, to be accurate in your speech. But it carries this a step further by matching the speech to your intentions over time. It creates its own rhythm for your life. It allows you to be able to follow through with your intentions and also predict your ability to create outcomes. This makes you consistent, secure, and stable. It makes you optimal. It cultivates a beautiful rhythm of life that is not full of highs and lows and fits and spurts.

This is why following Commitment Four is important—because otherwise you can end up being conditioned by every piece of stimuli: peoples' emotions, what they are doing, and their communications. While you don't need to go against the grain of what everybody else is doing, you do need to follow your intentions and have your whole Self as you move through life so you end up co-creating with others instead of being hijacked all the time. Going back to the party example, you can attend and have a good time without being thrown off your intention to leave by 10:00 p.m. or only have one drink.

This Commitment needs to be understood deeply because one of the things humans have struggled with for eons is that they end up being ruled by their reactions. This is especially true for more emotionally sensitive people, who can get caught in reactive cycles because they feel so deeply. They aren't used to the power they have when they really utilize their creative capacity.

WHY BEING PASSIVE OR REACTIVE ISN'T AN OPTION

Some people who operate at a lower frequency might think it's easier just to react to life; they think they can't be blamed for what they do if they aren't actively creating anything. For many people, being in the power of their choices—just being a person who actively chooses—is, first of all, one level of emotional conditioning.

Here's another common example: You want to make your marriage better. You and your wife haven't been connecting, and it stresses you out. Reactivity causes people to create more of what they don't want. If you want to be closer to your spouse, a reactive person might spurt out their hurt, yelling, *You never talk to me, you don't care about me, you don't want to be close to me.* How do you think your wife will respond?

But reactivity is a captivated state of being, and it's a conditioned state that does not yield anything other than more of itself. It creates even more distance between you two. *If you're not paying attention to me, then I don't pay attention to you,* you think about her.

Reactivity is infectious. When someone yells, you're more likely to yell; if they are quiet, you're more likely to be quiet. It can feel like the most tempting thing to just lean into that reactivity and be swept away with it. While it may feel satisfying in the moment to do so, it won't get you to your outcomes.

But with intention, you say what you *do* want and what you want more of: *I just love living life with you. I'm inspired to live it more fully with you. I'd love to share more with you.* Your wife is far more likely to react well to this approach.

Another example: if you say, *I'm not going to drink alcohol,* then right there you've started the process for that drink to happen. But if you say, *I'm going to be so healthy, and my head is going to be clear. I'm going to drink orange juice, green juice, green tea, water, and seltzer,* you then have the process of what is already going to occur in motion.

This is not the same as suppressing yourself. It is all about harnessing your emotions and energy, especially the most intense ones.

Reactive cycles feel captive, like you can't stop yourself from doing them. Addiction can appear to be about drugs, pornography, or whatever else a person does compulsively, but it's really about being captive to reactivity—and that reactivity being so out of control that somebody needs more and more of it to feel anything, which has them overindulging. And that chain of reactivity keeps getting built every single time. The person feels something similar, and then they do it again and again. And it just becomes its own conditioning process.

I've worked with many people with addictions, and it feels to them like they are being swept away. Even though they don't want to drink, they end up drinking, and their lives keep spinning out of control. This is because when you talk about what you're not going to do, like, *I'm not going to drink for the rest of my life,* you already start the cycle for that happening because you are actually communicating that intention.

THE PAST = GOING BACKWARD

The reason why this Commitment is so impactful and effective is because it allows you to move every single thing in your life forward instead of living in a reactive state where you keep reprocessing your previous experiences and therefore recreating them.

Going to the past all of the time is what puts people behind. It's what causes people to have less, to be in a scarcity mindset, and have a lot of difficulty manifesting because they are literally living it within their own mind and being. They were often conditioned for it because the people they grew up with, their spouse, or who they're around now are in this mindset as well, so they co-create more of it. Eventually, the person feels increasingly uncomfortable because it's creating a compounding effect of going further backward in the wrong direction, getting more and more used to living in the past.

There are billions of people, and unfortunately some will continue to just constantly reprocess the past through the way they speak and act (and not even realize they're doing that) because it passes for what unfortunately is normal for how people communicate with themselves and each other.

With enough of this negative momentum, eventually someone is just behind in everything—in their development, creating what they need, or behind on their bills. That sense of being behind keeps creating more of itself. It's a trap where people will keep talking about it and doing things that are a reflection of that. People don't realize how powerful they are in creating this, even though they don't want it.

Say and do only what will create your outcomes—and say them out loud. When we send energy forward, it doesn't mean we always have to be straining or pushing really hard. It just means we get used to giving energy some direction. Then on a physical level, a material level, you create it. And so it's either going to be that you expand what you don't want with your attention toward it, or you expand what you do want with your communication about it.

This is an infinite field of possibilities, and you get to create your focus. All the materials you use that are in the atmosphere are within you as well. They're available now for everybody on the internet. They're in our imagination and on Earth. They are yet to be thought of, but you'll think of them and come up with beautiful ideas.

When you make the shift, and your communication to yourself and other people is about what you're going to do and how you're going to use what's happening to create something that you want, then that mechanism keys rolling. It keeps getting easier and easier. You become conditioned for that focus. You exist as a productive person, which really means that you're producing what you intend rather than producing more of what you don't want. This momentum is creating things for you so that they're happening and you don't have to constantly grind it out all the time.

Often our collective is an intentionality. It represents the things that we feel are absolutely what we mean to create as a society at that point in time and all of the things that are the opposite of that. Or it's the amount of energy and time that we are in the negative paradigm: What we fear. What we don't want. What we're afraid will happen. Your reality—and the reality we all share—is a reflection of our emotional reality.

With terrible things like poverty and crime, our big opportunity here is to recognize that just because they exist as reference points—because they were creations of what people have done with their attentions and their beliefs—we must have emotional strength to have our attention and our communications on what we want and to move ourselves through those issues.

Otherwise, we are in a trap where we stay stuck. We fear crime and judge it rather than understanding the way it was created and shifting how we see it, by first shifting it within our own emotional infrastructure.

You can take the goodness in the world and amplify it, no matter how small the gesture. You can acknowledge that someone handed you a shopping cart at the store, and a driver let you into their lane on the way back home. When you focus on what is working and what is abundant, all of that keeps creating more of itself and replaces the negative things. It's a very important aspect for you to see what is being gained all the time, even in the darkest of situations.

Collectively, we have violent, negative, angry feelings about a life of scarcity and lack, of horrible things. When in reality, all of that is created by our powerful creative mechanism that has the ability to create anything that it wants, including abundant opportunity and material wealth and well-being for everyone. Even that as a continual conversation of what you want to create, every single bit of that will create it. It takes all of us—everyone who reads this book, implements these Core Commitments, and shares this with as many people as possible—so that everyone is connected to the process.

COMMITMENTS QUESTION: What good things are happening in my life that I can focus on and amplify?

It may seem like trying to stay in intention all the time is really difficult. While it does take some work to make this your new conditioning, it's also a game-changer because by you carrying out this emotional framework, you can be you without feeling like you have to have a responsibility to change every single thing about everyone else in order to change it for yourself.

People are unhappy living with mixed result and living below their potential. This is the shift that allows that to happen so you're living in purpose virtually all the time. *Instead of seeing what you don't have, you train yourself to see how amazing life really is*—the beautiful flowers your neighbor planted, the thoughtful thing your spouse did without fanfare. Magnify everything good that you see so that everything you do has this multiplying process going on.

The same goes for what you have in your bank account too. Instead of saying, *I don't have much money,* talk about what you have, how much you have, and how much you have done, as a way of amplifying it.

When you make this shift, the things you notice can then inspire you—you see a bright red car as you walk and decide to get a bouquet of roses for your spouse, who then is extra attentive and kind to you, elevating your relationship even more. The process is a continual inspiration that keeps leading to more fuel and energy.

I invite you to "flip the switch"—move away from the societal tendency to focus on what isn't and move into a positive paradigm so you are receiving life, instead of living in lack and trying to eke out some life that you want. If you can't speak about what you want to yourself or others, or behave in the way that it is there, you can work your tail off and still keep re-experiencing the same exact lack, struggle, and scarcity because that is your conditioning. And this is why people work so hard and do so much, and yet their paradigm is for seeing what's wrong and their conversations are there for what isn't with themselves and others; their behaviors are based on what isn't happening.

Instead of saying, *I don't want to go to the dentist*, you say, *I want to have a bright, healthy smile.* That changes the whole experience of a mundane task, and you already created the experience before it happened.

COMMITMENTS QUESTION: How do I want to change the conditioning of my life?

When we have a specific vision of what we'd like to achieve with other people, it doesn't necessarily mean it will unfold exactly the way we see it—and that's okay. The key is to stay open and collaborative with others. If you want to take a trip with a girlfriend but you can't agree on where to go, you can say, *I really just want to go somewhere where we can relax and catch up with each other.* And then she can say, *That sounds really nice, and I'm also really wanting to get some shopping in,* then you can start to come up with places that will satisfy both needs and choose your destination. Your friend can add her intentions to yours. And now, you're in a creative process together where you keep inspiring each other. This goes for any partnership, including business deals.

In reality, being intentional and having specifics is what we're here to do, and other peoples' job is to do the same. And when we do it, we don't have to do it *for* them. They sync up with us. This is a tremendous change that happens. Just by you reading this book and implementing these Commitments, you'll be inspiring other people around you to be intentional too.

People generally want many of the same outcomes, and there's variations that make us unique. You'll find that your own intentionality feels so good to other people that they want to say "yes" to it and add their intentions until it goes from being "my" or "your" intentions to "our" shared intentions—a beautiful, integrated combination of our co-intentions and our co-creation that can only come from connected intentionality.

The things in life we enjoy have been created with intentionality. A wonderful meal was intentionally created by a chef, a beautiful building envisioned by an architect. They didn't say, *I don't want to eat this* or *I don't want my building to look like this.* And the things that cause suffering were created by reactivity. You have the power to make this shift so that the reality you experience is the one you intend and that you communicate. You recognize the powerful creator that you are of your reality. And when you do this, you create that reality for everyone else in the world to share in as well, just as others do for us.

This is the truth about the human condition: we get to condition it into whatever we want it to be. There is nothing static about it, and you are not stuck in whatever circumstances you have. You are here to expand from where you are into what you want it to be. You are here to focus on exactly what that vision is, and that is the way that you're going to create it. When this is your existence 24/7, that becomes who you are.

You have not yet seen all that you are capable of. Before, you were creating with maybe 10 percent of your capacity. And you were creating a lot of things in the most unfortunate way through your reactive capacity that you may not have recognized. But now, life is yours for the taking. It's truly yours to create. No matter how much negative conditioning you've absorbed, or how dysfunctional the patterns you've been at the effect of, this is your moment—and you can create anything you want.

Conclusion

IN 2011, A PALLIATIVE NURSE IN AUSTRALIA NAMED Bronnie Ware published a book called *Top 5 Regrets of the Dying*. Ware cared for people who were in the last twelve weeks of their lives, and she found that the things they regretted were remarkably similar. The most common one was *I wish I'd had the courage to live a life true to myself, not the life others expected of me.*

You now have the tools so that you will never have to experience this regret at the end of your life, or any day before that.

The other regrets people experienced, according to Ware, were:

- I wish I hadn't worked so hard

- I wish I'd had the courage to express my feelings

- I wish I had stayed in touch with my friends

- I wish that I had let myself be happier

These feelings were universal, regardless of gender, income, or other factors.

Although we are all different, there's so much about the human experience that is the same. We all want to be happy, healthy, loved, and living life in purpose. We want to be close to God, or Source, or the universal energy—however we envision our spiritual side.

You might feel broken or discouraged by what you've inherited from previous generations—medical issues or emotional issues. Although these are the legacy passed down to you, you are not these patterns. And the best legacy you can leave those you love is connected, intentional living.

Whether we realize it or not, we are all building a legacy. Some people do this deliberately from an early age; others will start to think about it once they have a heart attack or a loved one dies. And sadly, some will run from the idea no matter what, afraid that their life isn't important.

But you know now that your legacy is something you build moment by moment. It doesn't have to mean doing something highly publicized, either. Our thoughts, actions, and energy are all contributing to the collective experience. If you smile and open a door for someone else, that's part of your legacy. So too are your career, your family, and your community.

Your legacy is not only in the memory of people who might talk about you and think about you, but it is literally in a web of emotional influence and impact that happened from every single moment that you made a shift and implemented these Commitments. And when you said and did only what created the outcomes that you intended, and you lived in this vision. You funneled it through everything that you expressed in an action, in deeds, and in words. And it came through every single item in your life, everything you ever created.

And therefore, what is so exciting about The Commitments is that as people have the conditioning to fear death as if it is the end, and we fear that we won't exist anymore, these Commitments are the way in which we can be infinite.

We can be part of cycles that are created forward, that continue generation after generation with no end to our existence. We can be part of cycles that have meaning, purpose, and impact, and that continue to create the world well after our physical body shuts down.

When you know that, and when you live that every day, there is no end to what you can create in this world in such a limitless way.

There comes a peace with this and a prosperity for life. And even though The Commitments take some effort to become effortless, at their essence, they are simple and practical. I invite you to be in this life now, to co-create it, envision it, imagine it, construct it, and live in every aspect of it in each moment.

We are driving cars that somebody thought of, and we are eating food that somebody decided to crossbreed to be heartier and tastier. And this is the reality of being a human—that it is powerful, that we have great influence so far beyond anything we can see, feel, or be aware of, but that is as real as anything.

And it's either believing a reality that we have zero influence and very little control over anything or recognizing that we have power over *everything*. It's about deciding to use that power to live in it and create what we intend. And that is the incredible emotional-strength effect of every one of these Commitments.

There's no question, *Can I do it?* All of this conditioning of doubts and whether or not somebody can do something, this question doesn't even apply—as it never really did. *You know now that everything is possible and there is nothing in your way, other than your previous conditioning, which you're now committed to shifting and creating new conditioning.*

I invite you all to take these Commitments to yourself and deepen them. Accept this invitation and give to yourself and all of us every bit of what you are here to give and to receive. We all want to experience the "you" that you truly are and the full effect of everything you are here to contribute.

Further Resources

Now that you've learned *The Commitments* and have started to experience their life-altering power through daily practice, where do you go from here?

The first answer is to keep doing exactly what you're doing! The Commitments are about creating the destinations you want, but they are equally about the journey of life. They will help to guide you, from one moment to the next, for as long as you use them.

The second answer is to move from this book to practical action that can transform you at the highest level with more support, leadership, and guidance. You can up-level your commitment to your Self by giving yourself the emotional strength training that is designed to build up your capacity for intentionality. This will make your desired outcomes a reality that much faster and more effectively in your everyday life.

You can start by going to my website, www.DrTracy-Inc.com. There, you can learn more about me and my talented team. And when you visit the Work With Me tab, you'll see the many programs my company offers to help you with your biggest challenges. Whether it's addiction, relationship problems, anxiety or depression, overwhelm, or you just want to function at your highest level, we have the tools for you.

For a solo, self-empowered experience to put The Commitments into action, I recommend the Dr. T Solution. This is the most cost-effective way to access all of my teachings—of which The Commitments are only part.

You can also opt for the VIP Group Transformation Program, which teaches my methodology in an intimate group setting with my coaches.

And for the ultimate experience, my company offers an Exclusive Private Customized Transformation Program for the most personalized program and fastest results.

If your marriage is struggling or needs a tune-up (and really, whose doesn't?), I suggest the Marriage Transformation Program.

If you or a loved one are struggling with addiction—and are sick of methods that don't help—I highly recommend the Addiction Intervention Program. For even quicker results, we also offer a private, customized Recovery Retreat.

But really, the way to find out which program is best for you is by booking a free consultation call with a member of my world-class team.

I promise you that this thirty-minute call will be life-altering—it's really an intention session that allows our team to see your patterns, reactions, and intentions, and then offer a recommendation for a transformative program with us.

We can't wait to meet you.

Yours in intention and love,

Dr. T

Acknowledgments

The Commitments is a true collaboration that was created so magnificently because of the intentionality of the entire team at Dr. Tracy Inc.—a team that is the foundation allowing us to elevate the lives of so many people with our emotional training products and services. It is through the power of our amazing team that I've been able to bring forth the Commitments as a powerful tool to transform the lives of millions of people from reactive to intentional, and the team at Dr. Tracy, Inc. is at the heart of what makes this possible.

Bringing *The Commitments* to life has been one of greatest and easiest collaborations of my career due to the excellent creative process with Dr. Tracy Inc.'s Director of Content, Erica Patino. Erica's leadership was a dream turned into a reality for an author. Erica's ability to organize, translate, articulate, and elevate this book is on a world-class level, and her contribution has made it possible for so many people to integrate the Commitments into their lives and make significant changes that will have lasting positive impacts. It is Erica's beautiful balance of purpose and productivity that I'm always in awe of. I'm deeply grateful to Erica for everything she has done to make authoring books an enjoyable and streamlined process that makes it possible for us to help more people have the tools they need to succeed.

I also want to thank my husband Bruce, who is the ultimate partner in this purpose-driven life that we lead together. On our first date, I fell in love with him when he said he wanted to create a relationship that would inspire others. Once he added that "failure wasn't an option," I knew we would powerfully create an exceptional life together. Throughout our relationship, it's been the Commitments that have made it possible to navigate together through all of life's twists and turns, even more committed to transforming lives together. Through every reaction we've ever shifted into an intention, and through every intention that we've ever made into a creation, we make it possible for other people and their families to do the same. It's because of my husband's commitment to living our purpose together that *The Commitments* could be created and so many people can now enjoy it. Thanks to Bruce for being my partner because more than anything I love being the "Bunny" in our "Honey and Bunny" power-couple program.

It is with the deepest gratitude that I also acknowledge Master Coach Christina Ray, one of my greatest partners in life. Christina embodies purpose in both the overarching sense of a life of service to something greater than herself as well as in day-to-day interaction that we share and in everything I get to see her do. Christina demonstrates commitment and intentionality at every level. She is a world-class expert in keeping intentions at the forefront of everything she does, and she shifts reactions into intentions with the top capacity of anyone I've encountered. She is both love and power in an exquisite combination that allows our company to help highly reactive people transform into the most intentional people on the planet. Witnessing Christina lead herself, her family, our company, our clients, and our community, is to witness a great masterpiece in the form of a person. It's like being a fashion designer seeing a stunning model rock their clothing down the runway and make it look better than they could have imagined. Christina is both a muse and a master of intentional life creation.

Dr. Jenny-Viva Collisson—affectionately referred to as Dr. Viva—deserves major props for her contribution. She is one of the strongest people I know, and from the beginning, I knew that her purpose was as big as they come and that she would fulfill it. I also knew we were meant to create masterpieces together and to share a fabulous, fun life doing things that only the most purposeful people get to do. Having her as a collaborator is one of the most important things that's ever happened in my life because she cares about people at the highest level that allows all of us on our team to lead people "all the way" into their most intentional life. Dr. Viva is a stellar physician who embodies every possible definition of a transformative practitioner who gets the results for people with the most direct route to enlightenment, optimization, and high-performance living. As we share the purpose of intentional life creation, we also get to share the joy of birthing new lives for people that they never thought possible. While these transformations bring out the strength, love, and power at the core of

Dr. Viva, it is also her trademark humor and laughter that makes partnering with her an epic success.

This book was made possible due to the courageous clients of Dr. Tracy Inc. who commit so fully to their intentions and to living out their most elevated lives. They make a commitment that very few people ever do: to spend a year transforming all of their sensitivity and reactivity into intentionality and into the most elevated emotions, outcomes and incomes. By going from being reactive to intentional, they are changing the paradigm of the whole world—for themselves, their families, and their professions. It's because of these clients that I am that much more committed to making transformation easy for people.

I always have in mind the children of our team members at Dr. Tracy Inc. and the children of our clients who have inspired this book and all of the transformative intentions of the Dr. Tracy Inc. company. I want to acknowledge all of these youngsters for implementing the principles of this book and showing that training for intentionality can never start too early. Witnessing the kids transform through being in intentional families with intentional parents and seeing them prosper beyond the reactivity that they once had to navigate brings the most joy to my heart and moves me to bring my emotional training Method and the Commitments to the world.

I want to acknowledge my husband's family, the McGoverts, who have one of the strongest commitment to family that I've ever seen. They are another layer of the foundation that allowed me to create because they support Bruce and me and what we create with Dr. Tracy Inc., including this book. Thank you to all of the McGoverts for sharing Bruce with me.

I also want to recognize my grandfather John. He was a role model for commitment to family. He took total responsibility for his role as a leader of the family and carried that all the way out through his life. He said to me, "Out of all of my family members, I never worry about you because I know you're always going to be successful," which was the highest compliment I can imagine, and his belief in me has allowed me to elevate the lives of many people.

There's another important being who helped me, too: my dog Lola, who was much more than just a pet; she was my furry daughter. She lived over half her life with a debilitating injury, but her entire presence was all about intentionality, and she just moved forward in everything with fervor. Her commitment was to keep being there for me for as long as she could, living far longer than predicted. This will always be a great example of what is possible when one focuses on their intentions.

I want to acknowledge all of my mentors, colleagues, and collaborators who have contributed to my growth and the growth that led to this book coming to life. So many incredible people have supported my vision to provide a full-scale range of solutions and services that support the world's most Emotionally Sensitive people to be able to build the emotional strength that they need to succeed. In a world where Emotionally Sensitive people can feel chewed up and spit out by all the reactivity they experience, this range of supporters have validated, encouraged, and helped me carry out my vision—especially this book, which is a love letter to those who struggle with emotional sensitivity and reactivity.

One of these mentors is Russ Ruffino, a role model for how to create something bigger than yourself that other people get to benefit from immensely. Russ has given people the ability to live their dreams and take care of their families, and it was an incredible help to be able to follow in his footsteps.

Along with Russ, I want to acknowledge Marc Von Musser, who lights up the world and people who are deeply committed to living their purpose. Marc leads people to come through their negative patterns into their intentions and holds the space for growing in a dignified, celebratory, heartfelt manner. He's a brother in arms, and I trust him completely.

Another such person is Kathryn Porritt: at a time when I needed a mentor who saw how big my vision was and who understood my purpose, she helped me be bolder in my message that life is luxurious when you use your emotions for a purpose. She's a role model for commitment, and her belief in my mission is a major reason that this book exists.

And I can't acknowledge Kathryn without also thanking Heather Bucciano. Another powerful force of intentionality, Heather helped me stay grounded in my intentions to help more celebrities and influencers transform Emotionally Sensitivity into their greatest asset instead of their most challenging liability. The combination of Heather's commitment to me and her sense of humor helped me operate on a whole new scale for people with the highest levels of emotional sensitivity who needed me to create more solutions for them, like this book.

Another major contributor was Selena Soo, who helped me influence millions of people to transform their emotions with years of media articles that eventually led to authoring books and creating commitments between me and my clients that totally transformed their lives.

Also, much appreciation to Aurora Winter, who had me fulfill the commitment of doing my TED Talk and commit to creating more books and more impact. She provided strategic guidance at a very pivotal time in my life and career that allowed me to follow the intention of more public speaking, both on stage and on the page.

The Commitments is also a direct result of the influence of my family, whom I have been inspired by every day of my life to live as an Emotional Scientist, helping people transform their reactivity into intentionality, whatever the circumstances, scenarios, or situations that they experience. It is because of my love for my family and all clans who want to live intentionally together that I have committed my life to understanding how to create happy families who live out purposeful, successful lives together. This book is a direct result of their influence in my life and all that I've ever wanted for all of us.

First and foremost, it was my mom, Frances, who gave me the advice at a very young age to keep track of myself and make sure that I was on track for what I intended. My mom taught me about committing to be my best self instead of enduring the same struggles as other family members. The directions to "keep track" helped me stay checked in to my intentions throughout my lifetime and helped me to help others do the same. It was my mom's unwavering commitment to me and my purpose that has allowed me to create solutions like this book that help others do the same.

Another crucial influence is my dad, Duane, who chose to be my dad when I was very young. He made a commitment to both my mom and to me that taught me that commitments to our chosen family can be just as big (if not bigger) than commitments with our DNA family. This kind of commitment is a phenomenal one that only some people can make, to choose to commit to a child and the adult that they will become, for a lifetime. I want to acknowledge his support throughout my life—for never opting out of his commitment to be my dad. It's been the foundation of me being able to commit to and make the Commitments. He's always been there, and I know he always will be, while he's alive and in my future memories, as a dad who went all the way with me. This commitment from my dad is worth everything to me.

I'm also acknowledging my father, Mike, for the commitments that he lived out to his family in the face of emotional sensitivity and trauma for many years until his emotional difficulties severely downgraded his life. Through him, I saw that when people are committed to being successful together as a family, how much success can be created, how fun life can be, and how infinite the possibilities are. He role-modeled what it is to build a company where people can grow and do something purposeful. He showed me what it meant to create a real, material reality using intentions, commitment to family, and a deep desire to provide for those he loved the most. When my father was intentional for his family, he was at his finest, and when he was in reactivity, he taught me why I needed to create solutions for Emotionally

Sensitive people like him. It was my dad's capacity for success and his capacity for stress that has directed my purpose since my first memories. It is my love for him and the love I know he had for me that motivates me every day to create emotional training that puts people on track for their intentions and ensures they stay on track through their lifetimes.

And I want to acknowledge my Uncle Tommy, who has triumphed over some of the most challenging things I've ever seen happen to an Emotionally Sensitive, purpose-driven person. This propelled me to create the Method and the Commitments for Emotionally Sensitive people to thrive and bring all of their intentions into reality. Through the years that he worked to overcome addiction and reunite with his family, he inspired me to create something that could work for everyone and every family. It's his dedication to the recovery of himself, his family, and his contribution to helping so many other recovering people that inspires me. And his commitment to loving me, especially after my dad passed away, allowed me to transform grief into some of the greatest creations of my lifetime. It is also his commitment to receiving my love that helped me remain my higher Self through many shocking developments of what felt like a movie version of someone else's lifetime. It is the commitment to move forward together that I share with my uncle and allows me to share it with others.

My cousin McKensie is another person I'd like to thank for her commitment to me and to our family. Commitment is the number-one word I'd use to describe my cousin, who is more like the sister I've always wanted and someone I know will continue to be there with me throughout my lifetime. She's a leader, a role model for our family, and I want to be more like McKensie when I grow up! With all of the struggles that can occur in a family, each one needs a person who prioritizes the commitment to stay together. Through tragedy, loss, and trauma that our family has endured, McKensie's compassion for everyone is the commitment that creates the possibilities for who we can be in the future instead of being defined by our past. It is this commitment that we both share to a brighter future together that helped me create the Commitments.

I also want to thank my lifelong friends and the friends who feel like they've been with me my whole life. They are a big part of the foundation that has allowed me to lead and live my purpose. It is these friends who support me and who make it possible for me to do that for other people. This is what they have done for me throughout my life, always seeing the best in me, and in any moment of challenge, they've always provided the grace for me to grow and the knowledge that my place with them is always secure. They have given me great comfort and strength and have been a source of much laughter, silliness, and happiness through it all. My dear friends have made friendship and commitment synonymous, and this has been one of the greatest luxuries of my life. Because of the commitments, my friends have shown me I know what commitment means in real life.

I'd like to acknowledge the Dr. Tracy Inc. community of fans and followers engaging with us across all our media channels, including YouTube, Facebook, our newsletters, and our books. They are an inspiration for stepping up, tuning in, and following and implementing all of the emotional training that I put into the world to help be their most intentional selves. Through their questions, comments, and commitment to living their most elevated lives, the community has spurred me to create this book—and another one that's almost done—because of their hunger for training and growth that is so powerful. It is our community that continually shows their dedication to emotional transformation, which encourages all of my creations.

Thanks to our publishing team at Scribe Media, who helped us bring forward our manuscript and make it into the book of our dreams so we could get these Commitments to people who really need them. To Rose Friel and Mikey Kershisnik, our dedicated Publishing Managers, who kept us on track and inspired us to get this book out in record time. And to our graphic designer, Anna Dorfman, who helped us bring the cover design to life so the book exudes all the luxury and class that people feel when they follow the Commitments.

Last but not least, to the Emotionally Sensitive people of the world who may have, up to this point, believed that there was something wrong with them and that their sensitivity is a liability: I'm here to tell you that it is your greatest asset. When sensitivity is not well understood, it can seem like a burden. But the Emotionally Sensitive strive through it, and they show the world that it needs to become more emotionally evolved so we can all live in an emotionally elevated and high-intentional environment. I acknowledge the world's most Emotionally Sensitive, intuitive, multisensory, empathic people for being the greatest inspiration and the greatest community and the people who are here to change the world through bringing the combination of sensitivity and intentionality together. I love them. I thank them. And I'm committed to create more for them throughout my lifetime. They are courageous, incredible, and powerful creators who are building a better world for everyone with every intention they live out and every reaction they retire.

To these Emotionally Sensitive beings: I see who you really are, and most importantly, I see who you are here to be. Step into that purpose, and it will lead you forward into your destiny and your ultimate legacy.

CPSIA information can be obtained
at www.ICGtesting.com
Printed in the USA
BVHW090922040222
627409BV00009B/174/J